I can't take one more thing!

I can't take one more thing!

Aggravated Assault On Your Mind

Parice C. Parker

I can't take one more thing!

Aggravated Assault On Your Mind

Copyright © 2013 by Parice Parker. All rights reserved.

No part of this publication may be reproduced, stored in a retrieval system or transmitted in any way by any means, electronic, mechanical, photocopy, recording or otherwise without the prior permission of the author except as provided by USA copyright law.

Scripture quotations, unless otherwise indicated, are taken from the *Holy Bible, King James Version*, Cambridge, 1769. Used by permission. All rights reserved.

The opinions expressed by the author are not necessarily those of Fountain of Life Publisher's House.

Published by Fountain of Life Publisher's House

P. O. Box 922612, Norcross, GA 30010
Phone: 404-936-3989
Please Email Manuscripts to: publish@pariceparker.biz
For all book orders including wholesale email:
sales@pariceparker.biz
To request author email: author@pariceparker.biz
www.pariceparker.biz

Fountain of Life Publishing House is committed to excellence in the publishing industry. The Company reflects the philosophy established by the founder, based on Psalm 68:11, "The Lord gave the word and great was the company of those who published it."

Book design copyright © 2013 by Parice Parker. All rights reserved.
Cover Design by Parice Parker
Interior design by Phyllis R Brown
Editor: Phyllis R Brown

Published in the United States of America

ISBN: 978-0-978-716233

Library of Congress TXu1-215-737

Date: February 13, 2016

I can't take one more thing!

Aggravated Assault On Your Mind

TABLE OF CONTENTS

Introduction..6

Preface..9

1. What is the Use...10

2. When Strong Winds Blow....................................30

3. Endure Your Life Assaults....................................61

4. What Are You Feeding Your Mind..................... 90

5. Future Effects of Breaking Through.................133

6. Mark me and be Astonished..............................163

7. Dwelling in Safety...179

8. Stop the Aggravations..195

9. Throw Some Stuff Overboard...........................215

I can't take one more thing!

10. No Weapon Formed..239

11. God's Word is Your Defense..........................264

12. Skin for Skin..283

13. Wash Your Steps with Butter........................303

14. The Return of Captivity.................................321

Parice C. Parker

I can't take one more thing!

Aggravated Assault On Your Mind

Introduction

Have you ever felt that the very person you have surely loved or believed in has attacked you? It may have been your closest friend, relative, child, your spouse or even yourself. Sometimes you wanted to cry, and could not. Shortly afterward, while contemplating on the pain, immediately tears began to fall as a flowing river. Your heart assaulted and snared with claws of intentions to kill. A multitude of thoughts circulate in your mind, and then you began to say to yourself. "How did I let this happen to me?" Your situation was bound to occur, because somewhere along the way you have allowed your circumstance to control your mind. Allegedly, you put your trust in the wrong one or thing, and then you are thrown off guard.

You wonder, who do I blame? You did not

I can't take one more thing!

realize you had entrusted your heart to be assaulted through the passion of love; you had given. Blindness has overwhelmed your thinking ability, rearranging your life, and throwing it off balance. Truly, there is an explanation and an apology due. But, none is ever given. Indeed, you have tried to generate an effective change. Perhaps, the more you tried, the more your relationship seemed to die. And, you instantly think, what is the use?

Parice C. Parker

I can't take one more thing!

Aggravated Assault On Your Mind

"The one thing you need to keep in mind is if you do not get through this, then you will never get to your destiny!"

~Parice C. Parker

I can't take one more thing!

Aggravated Assault On Your Mind

Preface:

I have had to endure many afflictions, just to be able to write this book. There are inspirations our Heavenly Father intends for those that are struggling to sustain. At times, struggling can become overwhelming. Some have been trying their best to remain faithful during terrible times of conflict. However, they are brutally attacked in every area of their lives and often feel that they are spiritual assassinated. I was intensely aggravated as my faith was put on trial! One day, I realized my struggles were purposed for many to be set free. So, therefore, on this writing journey my heart desired to deliver the ones that had been under extreme spiritual attack. As you read this book, your heart will be richly enlightened as your mind will be spiritually renewed. Your life will never be the same, after finishing this book!

I can't take one more thing!

Aggravated Assault On Your Mind

CHAPTER 1
What Is The Use?

> *"Stop letting people use you, and your situations abuse you!"*
> ~Parice C. Parker

I can't take one more thing!
CHAPTER 1

What Is The Use?

Trouble here, trouble there; it seems that every door I knock on, trouble is everywhere. I know, it's all because of... Have you ever tried to help people that don't care about helping themselves? And, the more you try, the harder you fall. It is simply not fair! It is hard living a productive life when so many things, and people are holding you back. I can't count all that tried to hinder me. It only just breaks your heart, when your trying is not enough but I realized you just cant help everybody. Some you must leave alone. I know, because of the many bad experiences I have had. Often our hearts will harden and burdened because of life's aggravations. Still allow your heart to love others. Desire your promises enough to move forward and to be moved! Understand and do not let the same

I can't take one more thing!

people continue to hurt you. Just pray for them. *(Matthew 5:44)* Things will get better! Even though you're trying but haven't gotten to your destination yet, just keep on trying. Know that this too shall pass. Perhaps, you have had to go through, just to get to. Know that you are on your way! *Psalms 23:5, "Thou preparest a table before me in the presence of mine enemies: thou anointest my head with oil; my cup runneth over."* Many nights I laid awake and cried until no more tears could fall from my eyes. Surely, you are not alone! When you truly find yourself in need, it will not be a man that will help you out. Some are trying to bury you alive. Look around and keep watch on who you are surrounded by. They will fool you! I thank God that I had the opportunity to experience the truth of His love in my life. Never let how others mistreat you cause you to mistreat people. Always be prepared to let love spread throughout your heart. *(Proverbs 8:17)* However, if there is a problem then get away from those people. They are killing you! Sometimes you just need to walk away.

At one time in my life, I was the co-pastor of a

I can't take one more thing!

congregation that did not want to understand The WORD, no matter what. I struggled with people that did not care about their own soul's salvation. Also, many *despitefully* used me. Yes, you know those women that come to church, but not for Jesus. What about the ones that say, "God told me this and God told me to do that." Well, I found out the hard way. God might have told them, but they sure did not listen. Many are like that even today. What about those that continued to use you just because? Many have used Jesus too! However, that was one road I had to take for me to receive the right direction I was destined to go in. One day, I couldn't take it anymore, and I needed to be humble, especially after dealing with all that I had to. *(Matthew 18:4)* Yes, I had to walk away. One night in Bible study I realized that I first had to help myself. Not trying to sound selfish, but how can you help someone else if you can't even help yourself. My children were greatly in need of so much, and my family suffered from the abuse of people that did not care. Surely, I had to humble myself. A compromise was not an option for me. *(1 Peter 5:6)* I simply woke

I can't take one more thing!

up after many years of serving this bunch of people. God purposely begin to isolate me to speak soundly to my heart. He begins to prepare me for greater. I felt I was used, and my heart was wounded. Thank God that wounds do heal. Though many others cannot begin to love you in the way you need to be loved, God will. *Proverbs 8:17, "I love them that love me; and those that seek me early shall find me."* Though situations in your life seem to bring greater pressures on you, be patient. Just continue looking for a WORD from the Lord. Keep your eyes open. *Corinthians 14:33, "For God is not the author of confusion, but of peace, as in all churches of the saints."*

Often, we do not realize the many different opportunities in life we can live. People and things will burden you, but allow your spirit to be lifted. If you think for a moment and take notice of the wrong choices you have made, the many life aggravations that we have encountered have caused us all to do some form of a hard time. How much further did it draw you away from your goals? Also, how did the distance begin to grow between you and God? The

I can't take one more thing!

enemy loves to cause confusion and for many years, he has enjoyed every bit of it. Would it be great if we had a chance to do it all over again, or turn the clock back? How many things would you change if you had the opportunity? Your life is valuable, stop what is not right and begin something new. Probably, more than you can ever count, just one change could have caused you to be in a better position. Well since there is no chance to go back in time and make those changes, let's begin with obtaining knowledge for today. When you obtain knowledge, you will better understand life. Making wrong choices, unfortunately, is a part of living, and the key is to learn from our mistakes so that we will not continue making the same ones over again. What is old is old and what is new is to come, let it arise! Allow your future to brighten your horizon. Leave the past in the past and begin making the right choices for your future today. You have a purpose of pressing forth, so move forward. Someone needs you and is depending on you to obtain victory in your life. They need to see you achieve, so they can receive freedom in theirs. Looking through your eyes as of

I can't take one more thing!

right now, you may feel there is no use. Visualizing through the eyesight of GOD, there is much required of you. You may be angry and feel that so many people have used you, especially those you love. Friends, family, and many others who are related to us have victimized us all. Let no one hold you in contempt any longer. It is simply not worth it! For years, I allowed the enemy to have his way in my life, all because I lived for man. Trying to prove to them, that I was called and chosen. The only one you need to show yourself to is The Almighty! You will never be able to please all men. Surely, if you give the enemy an inch, he will be more than your ruler!

I tried everything I could to satisfy friends, associates, family, church people and so many more. One day I realized no matter how good you are to some, they are still resentful. People are going to classify and view you how they want. Believe me, I know. Stop wasting your time trying to satisfy them. You will get hurt every time! I quit associating myself with people that made me feel less than human. Some thrive on making you appear less! Yes, sometimes I'd

I can't take one more thing!

rather get a little lonely than go through some of the things I had to encounter for the sake of others. *Psalms 24:7, "Lift up your heads, O ye gates; and be ye lifted up, ye everlasting doors; and the King of glory shall come in."*

The enemy has tried to change your focus, and he wants to destroy you. The enemy wishes to mislead you towards a life of insecurities. His plan is to change your direction, aiming to dilute your zeal for life's assurance. Yeah, that is right; he is trying to turn you off your course of righteousness. He wants to rearrange your goals. So, therefore, you will not achieve in life.

Mind Affliction is the greatest way the enemy has to destroy you, tearing at your mental abilities. The enemy is just trying to disable your future by locking down your mind. He wants to stop your progress, destroy your zeal and steal your future of prosperity. Walk on and lift your head, know where you are going in life. Know what you want and seek God for it until you receive it. Leave who you and get

I can't take one more thing!

to stepping. For years, I searched everywhere for freedom. I often thought it was with my husband, family, friends, and the church. I searched for love in all the right places, but in the wrong people and things. It sounds awkward, but it is true. It is people that the enemy will use to try and destroy us. Who are your friends, family members, and church associates serving? If it is the enemy, they will keep hell stirred up in your life. If it is a little hell and a little religion, then they will still not be faithful to you, because they cannot be faithful to Jesus. However, if they are true Jesus lovers, then they will be good to associate with, and they will keep you inspired. However, all I was searching for was already inside of me. I just had to allow Him to live greater in me, and I had to trust Jesus to be my God. I had to let Him deliver me from Aggravated Assaults on my mind! The more I allowed God to grow in me, meant less room for the enemy to assault my mind. By all means necessary, do what you need to get the hell out of your life! It's soul-threatening, protect your inheritance! *Psalms 24:5, "He shall receive the blessings from the Lord, and*

I can't take one more thing!

righteousness from the God of His Salvation."

The enemy loves confusion, and he is the author of it. *1 Corinthians 14:33* If the enemy can keep you confused about anything, then he can keep your mind unstable, and you will walk into disaster. His whole purpose is to aggravate your life by assaulting your mind first. His intention is to keep you walking blind! He does not want you to see further than life aggravations. You think that once you get over this and then overcome that, Satan is defeated. Satan wants your future, and prosperity indefinitely eliminated. He is trying to provoke you to sin. He wants to have control over your peace of mind. What the enemy means for your bad, God will and can turn anything around for your good. Regardless of what it is, only He has the power to do so! Allowing confusion to take over will keep you aggravated about your life. It is not worth another day to be confused, aggravated or irritated. God wants to give you peace of mind about everything in your life. Do not let life's aggravations stop you from seeking God. He is the only way to live in perfect peace, and once you

I can't take one more thing!

receive Christ, there is another soul that the enemy has lost.

If you look at our generation today, the enemy is causing chaos everywhere we turn. *Psalms 24:6* He is trying to affect everyone you love, and he is on a great mission of destruction. You must stay focused on God through it all. We cannot allow what the enemy is doing to destroy our faith. Sometimes in life, things just hurt, and when our life does not go as we planned, we get upset. This time, you must seek God, not be provoked by your situation or aggravation. When you seek God, it only means you need Him for a purpose. Let God know that He has a purpose in your life. Also, let the enemy know that you are not interested in his tricks or treats. God wants you to search for Him in every place you can, every decision you make and everything in your life. When you continue to search for God, you will find everything that you need. Many have found the Lord during their troubling times. However, Job knew Him before all his troubles aroused in his life. Those troubling times taught him more about God. He learned to trust in the Lord like

I can't take one more thing!

never before. He learned not to trust any man, but to pray for his enemies. Job learned many things from his many troubling experiences. In every hard time, God has a message for us all, and He wants us to listen. *Psalms 25:17, "The Troubles of my heart are enlarged: O bring thou me out of my distresses."*

He has the power to authorize an instant change in your life, which will bring the enemy to full correction about who you are. Stop allowing the enemy to use your life situations to upset your day. He wants to ruin your personality and cause you to live in a world of distress. I have personally seen many relationships ruined, because of aggravated assault on the mind. Some people have allowed their life aggravations which provoked them to fall into terrible situations. I have also seen relationships die, all because of life assaults that will cause irritations. Allow God to bring you out of stressful circumstances. Think of the day when you will receive double for your trouble. Oh, what a day that will be. Job had many people and things that tried to aggravate him. His friends and family put him down; they criticized

I can't take one more thing!

him and looked at him as though he did not trustworthy or righteous. Even his wife prosecuted him, just like many of us during our troubling times. Often, your spouse will give up on you or try to consume your faith. People are going to try all sorts of things to upset you and cause you mind confusion. However, do not let it destroy you. Job was prosecuted in every angle in his life and if he made it over, so can you. *Job 4:5, (Words of Eliphaz one of Job's friends) "But now it is come upon thee, and thou faintest; it toucheth thee, and thou art troubled."*

This appears familiar as you go through any form of life concerns; the first thing your friends or family do is begin to point the finger at you. Whatever it is that is bothering your mind, do not let it touch your heart. Eliphaz was one of Job's friends, and immediately he begins to discredit Job's worthiness to God because trouble had arisen in his life. Friends will surely do the same for you. That thing can only have power as you meditate on it because then you will feel the discomforts that it will cause in your life. I know this kind of aggravation personally. When trouble

I can't take one more thing!

arises in your life, someone is always prepared to point the finger at you. They will bring up a thousand and one excuses as to why trouble has appeared in your life and cannot handle their own. They always have all the wrong answers. Noticeably, in most cases, that is exactly what the enemy wanted many to think. He enjoys putting the pressure on someone, pointing the fingers at their faults so that particular individual can feel the pressures of their life. He intends to cause them to run to sin! Once you begin to feel the pressure, you will eventually begin to make irrational decisions that will affect the outlook of your life. Satan's purpose is to make you feel that you are not worthy of anything, and your life has no purpose. Eliphaz was not the first to prosecute Job. The enemy adores the fact when people look down on you because it decreases many from looking up towards God. Satan had beaten him to the punch. During critical moments, your heart can be easily crushed. Once the enemy begins to pressurize you, many people and things will begin to flee. Just fall and look to see who is around. They will run out of your life so

I can't take one more thing!

that you will not ask them for a favor. Hold on, God will remove things and people out of your life, just to give you a peace of mind. He will make things appear worthless in your life to many so that they can see His worth work through you. Someone always has to pay the price, and this time, I did not mind being that person.

Being purposely used is not always bad, just as long as God is using you. The funny thing I found out, the enemy could not stand his hell. Soon as hell rise in your life, all the horrible people will flee too. One of my favorite quotes, "Fall hard enough and see who's who!" The same ones that will run to you and ask you to pray for them will help push you over the edge. Now when I had it going on, business doing well, church growing and things happening, I can always hear them say, "That's my first lady, that's my pastor – ooh she can pray!" Well, I guess all that soon changed and I am glad it did. What the enemy purposed for my bad, God was just hand picking some people out of my life. After all, they never cared who needs a smile when the heart is black and who needs fake love when

I can't take one more thing!

we have JESUS. *Proverbs 8:17, "I love them that love me; and those that seek me early shall find me."* I knew that eventually God was going to give me double for my trouble. However, that was before I discovered about a hundred-fold return. We all will have a payday, and I was expecting double for my trouble payday from God. No matter what happens in your life, trust in Him. If you hold on to Him, He will never let you go. He loves you! I have never known Him not to be a Miracle Worker! Though you need your miracle right now, God is going to deliver you. He will not be a second too late. *Job 1:4, "and Satan answered the LORD, and said, skin for skin, yea, all that a man hath will he give for his life."* Satan wanted everything Job had because he knew the Lord had blessed him mightily. Satan noticed how much God appreciated Job's faithfulness, and adored the way Job respected The Almighty. Satan was trying to aggravate Job to the point that he would break away from God. Surely, Satan assaulted Job in every way. Hell surrounded Job and yes, it all was breaking loose in his life. Satan wanted Job to realize that God was not a

I can't take one more thing!

God of truth. He thought Job was one that he could fool by taking away his material things, and love ones. Sometimes many people have more love for their material possessions than they do God. However, Satan would soon realize that Job was not going to be separated from the love of his God. Satan occupation begins ultimate life assaults, by testing him in every angle of his life. Many of us will go through lost, but our hearts should never be wrapped up into material or worldly possessions greater than our Heavenly Father. We all know Job loved his children, even during his grief he had to love God. God gave Satan the privilege to strike everything Job loved, including his family but not his life. Satan has the power that God will only allow him. He may touch the things around you, but he cannot touch your life. Just remember, do not permit him more as life aggravations assault your mind. However, he can try to harm us all in many areas, in many things that surround us and through many people. Never let him have your soul! He might have some power, but Jesus has the greatest power of all. Job was assaulted for a purpose. Though times

I can't take one more thing!

were hard, he still served his purpose for God to gain more credit ability. Though the enemy thought it was more for his personal gain, it was all for God to receive the greater glory. Job's story is the most familiar that many preachers and teachers use as an example to express to the people during stressful times. Job is one of the Bible's greatest examples to hold onto your faith no matter what. *Philippians 3:15, "Let us therefore, as many as be perfect, be thus minded: and if in anything ye be otherwise minded, God shall reveal even this unto you."*

One thing God wants you to realize is that your life can change! Do you want the good things of life, because it is possible for you to obtain them? This thing that you are going through stop questioning yourself what is the use? Your mind must stay focused on Jesus. Your mind must be enriched with positive thinking, which will bring forth a positive life. You are everything to God, and He needs you to prove to Satan that you love The Almighty. *Proverbs 8:17, "I love them that love me; and those that seek me early shall find me."* You would be surprised on how many

I can't take one more thing!

people are looking up to you and praying for you. It is always someone you least expect that has his or her eyes on you. God needs you, and He wants to reveal your life purpose. Though it seems like you are worth nothing to many, you are worth greatness to God. He has so many wonderful things He wants to use you for and if you cannot find a use, believe me, He will. For every troubled time, you experienced, God is going to give you double for it, just as He did Job. *Philippians 3:16, "Nevertheless, whereto we have already attained, let us walk by the same rule, let us mind the same thing."* Sometimes the trouble will come our way that will cause us to get motivated in the Word. To many people you appear to be nothing, wasting time and a laughing joke. God will soon give them a revelation of who you are. So, do not worry about proving yourself to anyone but ?

I can't take one more thing!

Aggravated Assault On Your Mind

"Don't let the storm get the best of you, but get the best out of your storm!"

~Parice C. Parker

I can't take one more thing!

Aggravated Assault On Your Mind

CHAPTER 2
When Strong Winds Blow

"Don't let the storms toss you around!"
~ *Parice C. Parker*

I can't take one more thing!

CHAPTER 2

When Strong Winds Blow

Yeah Right, when storms roar – they say, "Don't Give Up – Hold On." How is it, when the forces of the wind are beating so hard, and you are about to fly away – everyone says Hold On? Sometimes it is hard to hold on when all you can think about is letting go. Just briefly thinking about Job and the friends he had as he was going through all his multiple trials. They could not inspire him with pure faith because they did not know the magnitude of being faithful. *Job 8:1&2 (Another friend of Job's),* "Then Answered Bildad the Shuhite, and said, How long wilt thou speak these things? And how long shall the words of thy mouth be like a strong wind?" How

I can't take one more thing!

could they possibly have told Job to hold on and wait on the Lord, if they had no spiritual soul-wrenching experience of knowing our Heavenly Father for themselves? They understood what it meant to hang on. When the forces of the high winds blow, you will not have time to think about what you are going to do next. That is why it is best to be grounded and rooted in the word. So, therefore, you can always be faithful, and if not that you can bounce back fast. High winds can blow your house down and cause destruction on every side. If your faith is not strong, you will just fall to pieces. The enemy tries you as the big bad wolf. He will try to huff and puff until he blows your house down. If your house (Mind) is not built solid as a rock, then He will demolish you and it. Your mind must be constructed solidly on The Rock, and The Rock must be inside of you. You must show your enemies what you are made of. Let them know that you are not going to be moved. Show them your Solid Rock Faith. *Deuteronomy 34:4, "He is The Rock, his work is perfect: for all his ways are judgment; a God of truth and without iniquity, just and right is He."* Through

I can't take one more thing!

many of my personal life experiences such as deeply troubled times, soul-stirring trials that have encountered my life through numerous sufferings, the wind blew harder and harder. It seemed as though my hands could not grasp fast enough to hold on. I know how it all feels when you get aggravated with life. You want things to happen, and you try with all you have, but the wind keeps forcing you down! Every time I built something, it seemed as though the wind blew harder against it. If I looked to the left, the storm was raging. When I looked at the right, the wind rose higher, and the winds grew more forceful. No matter how hard the wind blows, remember God is the only one with control over the wind. Sometimes it is the worst storms that will cause you to want to be grounded and rooted in God. You never know when a storm is coming towards you. Therefore, be prepared at all times.

Rock is something that is hard to break; it is solid. Diamonds come out of the stone, and many other precious stones are made from them. Rock has

I can't take one more thing!

boundaries. It stands firm on its foundation. Nothing can move a stone of great stature because the weight is substantial. It has been created never to blow in the wind. You must be grounded and solid as a rock. Being unmovable simply means that you stand firm and fast. Though the winds may try to shake you, just stand. Through many storms, houses may blow away, things will uproar as rooftops fly off, but the foundation is still in place. You will find great security in The Rock. Rock was not created to break, but through it all to be solid! So don't worry! *11 Peter 3:1, "The SECOND epistle, beloved, I now write unto you; in both which I stir up your pure minds by way of remembrance."* Understand that your mentality is one of your greatest and most vital assets of your human body. It must be made solid! Without the destruction of your mind, how can you possibly be destroyed? Your mental ability guides the direction of your life in the way you are destined to go. If your mind is irritated and afflicted through the many violent assaults that have come your way, then your life will dramatically change. It is either going to change for

I can't take one more thing!

better or worst. Which one would you prefer? If you reminisce on the wrongest, then eventually your life will blow into pieces. Certainly, your mind is what leads you towards decision-making. *Romans 8:28, "And we know that all things work together for good to them that love God, to them who are the called according to his purpose."* It enables you to gain knowledge and understanding of making the right or wrong choices in your life. Only you know what you want for your life because you are the only one that must live with it every second of the day. It is amazing how many of us have allowed others to keep confusion in our lives. I refuse to let someone make life decisions for me knowing that I am the one that is truly going to reap the benefits. You must be more than careful whom you allow in your life. *Proverbs 27:17, "Iron sharpeneth iron; so a man sharpeneth the countenance of his friend."* Be careful who you associate with. They can either help encourage you to become wiser or discourage you from becoming one of the life's greatest failures. Make sure your associates help complete the God in you. I made many

I can't take one more thing!

mistakes taking the wrong advice from the wrong people. Nevertheless, everything that sounds good is not always good advice. Neither is it the right advice for your life. I found out the hard way that it is so easy for someone else to give me advice on my life because they do not have to live with the consequences. It only takes a couple of minutes, perhaps seconds to receive the wrong information that will ultimately change your life. Every day I question myself, what is the use? Is the advice that I am receiving from a dear friend truly going to be profitable for God and me? Is the advice good advice that will cause me to walk mightily in the righteousness of God? Also, how is this personal information going to impact my life and affect my future and reflect The Highest? We all need to ask ourselves these three questions before we fully make any more decisions:

1. Are our lives representing righteousness at all times, regardless of the circumstances or conditions?
2. Do we possess, in our minds, every valuable element to succeed in this life? And

I can't take one more thing!

3. Are our mental abilities responsive, such as making the right decisions in our lives?
4. *Psalm 136:4, "To him who alone doeth great wonders: for his mercy endureth forever."*

Remember the many things God has done for you this year, things that you thought were just impossible. He has made ways out of no way for you, and some of you have not recognized that yet. Others of you have graciously thanked Him. Every day He has given you the power to wake up, be in your right mind and has allowed you to see another day. Figure this, multiply 365 days in a year times your present age; that is enough to glorify Him. This is a new day that He has made for you to have another life opportunity. He has allowed you to eat, sleep, live and has fed your family meals for all these years. Often we are so busy looking for a mighty miracle until we just cannot recognize the biggest miracles. It is a wonder and a blessing just to wake up day after day, to experience another life opportunity. You still have a chance to become all that you can become, through

I can't take one more thing!

the power of God. Perhaps, God intended you to feel exactly like you are feeling to stir up your mind so you can remember that He is God. I call it, a brewing spiritual effect from on high. I am not talking about a God of a little power, but the God of All Powers. *Matthew 28:18 says, "All power has been given unto me in heaven and earth," which caused Jesus to walk on the water and Jesus to heal the blind.* Jesus has the power over the enemy and possesses the rights to his territory. When God begins to stir things up, it becomes a powerful brew. Surely, you shall remember that He is who He is and know that He is God Almighty. *Psalms 121:8, "The LORD shall preserve thy going out and thy coming in from this time forth, and even for evermore."* As you go through, God is keeping you. I remember when I was little, my grandmother use to prepare her preserves for the winter. She knew how to make them. She packed them in jars; she was making her family pantry as well as stocking up on preserves. My favorite was her jelly preserves. I believe God does the same with us. Even as we go through our worst times, He is still

I can't take one more thing!

preserving us. I noticed the longer sweet preservatives sit, the more delicious the taste. The longer you handle what you are going through, the more generous your blessings will be. He preserves us before we enter and as we come out, just as He did Job. *Job 1:12, "And the LORD said unto Satan, Behold, all that he hath is in thy power; only upon himself put not forth thine hand."* Therefore, Satan went forth from the presence of the LORD. Even before Satan was able to have power over the things of Job's life, God preserved him going in and coming out. Just like those strawberry preserves that my grandmother prepared, they were sweeter after she preserved them. It is the same way Job's life was affected before his many aggravated assaults. *Psalm 121:8, "The LORD shall preserve thy going out and thy coming in from this time forth, and even for evermore."* His life was sweeter after he was ultimately delivered.

The enemy does not want you to be in full awareness of what God is and can do in your life. He does not wish you to give God total control. Because

I can't take one more thing!

as long as he can control just an ounce of your mind, then he can keep you upset, distraught and confused. He can keep you away from a blessed life full of happiness, joy and laughter. Your primary concern is going to be protecting your faith. By all means necessary, you must defend your faith. Because if you do not soon find a change in your mind's thinking ability through the power of God, it will trigger on down to your next generation of kin. One day I had the greatest wake-up call in my life. It was after I tried to continue with the ministry. My children had suffered dearly, but for all the right reasons. My husband and I sacrificed richly for the ministry and yes I am grateful to have experienced it all. It blessed us to give earnestly to Him. One day I looked up and realized, I am not Jesus. My children needed me more; I didn't want to continue in ministry and neglect my own. I believe God expects our eyes to open to our situations. Although our intentions were to help others, we were wearing ourselves out helping the wrong people. It's almost like giving a murderer a ride, thinking that you can't die. When you know that

I can't take one more thing!

danger is there, leave it alone. Don't play with your soul, it is like playing with fire. I was burdened at times; I felt like I was suffocating my praise, worship, and gifts. You must get away from the people and things that aggravate you, it's not worth it. Look at your children and find a use, stop questioning yourself about what is the use? However, if your mind is not aware of what is going on, then you are living as a human vegetable. Stop allowing aggravations to rob your household blessings. Our brain sends messages to every part of our body when the time needed for use. Let God take control of your mind. *Psalm 121:8, "The LORD shall preserve thy going out and thy coming in from this time forth, and even for evermore."*

Your mind is such a terrible thing to waste that is why the enemy always attacks your mind first. He tries so hard to consume all Godly authority over your life by afflicting your mind with such a little thought of sin. Sin will devastate your life forever if you act upon that particular idea. *Job 1:4, "And Satan*

I can't take one more thing!

answered the LORD, and said, Skin for skin, yea, all that a man hath will he give for his life."

The thing that has caused you to be so aggravated was for your life's Preservation Point. *Psalm 121:8, "The LORD shall preserve thy going out and thy coming in from this time forth, and even for evermore."* God will not keep something that is rotten, but rather someone He can use. God has preserved your future through the way you hope and just to incorporate a new way of thinking for you. God knew I was worth so much more than just being someone's punching bag or trash can. If my gifts are not properly being used, then how can God receive His proper glory? I no longer wanted to waste or distort my gifts. I needed to be around the ones that God knew would appreciate my gifts. Admittedly, many people do not understand what ministers must go through, especially first ladies. Our loads are so heavy, and no one ever stop to ask us "can I help you carry that load?" Truthfully, a first lady never gets the respect they deserve. Most people forget they are even there. When

I can't take one more thing!

I said, "My children needed me more, and then that's what I meant." I did not want to raise my kids to the point they would eventually hate church or God. *I Timothy 5:8, "but if any provide not for his own, and especially for those of his house, he hath denied the faith, and is worse than an infidel."* Our family needed balance and love. I wanted to continue ministering; I just changed the way I ministered. I begin ministering in books and music, as I was able to tend more to the needs of my young children. However, first the ministry God gave me had to begin in my home. I do not mind how people view me; I just want to satisfy my Lord. However, I am glad that I was not too proud to finally realize how much my babies needed more of their mother's affection, smiles, hugs, time, and love.

Sometimes we can get off guard by being there more for strangers than our own. However, which one would God prefer? He wants us to take better care of our homes. Just another way life can tend to get aggravated, by assaulting our peace in the home! The

I can't take one more thing!

choices we make will dearly affect our family and us.

Some people may have to do some hard time, locked up, and then others put on death row, all because of a wrong life choice and a wrong mindset. This assault on your mind may hurt, but it is intended for you to make up your mind and keep your mind on your life preservation point. There is a certain point in life that God wants you to reach, and it is your Preservation Point. He's been preserving your promises. In it is everything you will ever need. Whether you are bound, locked down, tied up, burdened down or shackled. No one is free until they reach JESUS. Through this assault on your mind, it has caused many to be afflicted. Look at your situation and notice who else is affected because of your situation. Remember, God is God over your going in, going through and your coming out. *Psalm 121:8 says, "The LORD shall preserve thy going out and thy coming in from this time forth, and even for evermore."* Just be patient during your stormy times. Trouble don't always last, praise The Lord! *Psalms*

I can't take one more thing!

90:7, "For we are consumed by thine anger, and by thy wrath are we troubled." Your mind conceives, and then it begins to act on what it conceives. Your mind is your personal library that informs the rest of your body on how to act, what to do and it gives your life an identity. Leading you as it guides you through your day-to-day decisions. At all times, you must keep your mind guarded through the feeding of intelligence, such as educating your mind with knowledge. As you gain experience, then you will have a good sense of understanding. *Ecclesiastes 2:26, "For God giveth to a man that is good in his sight wisdom, and knowledge, and joy; but to the sinner he giveth travail, to gather and to heap up, that he may give to him that is right before God.* This also is vanity and vexation of the spirit." Life is only what you help it to become. As you gain understanding, then you shall obtain wisdom. Your mind is the consumption tool to life's astringents. Your mind must stay in the right state to remain in an active functional mode. Your life controlled by the inhabitants of what you allow in your mind. After your mind receives a notion, it is

I can't take one more thing!

released throughout your body, generating an effect to progress. Your mind is either going to be in a healthy spiritual state or dysfunctional. Trouble comes, and it goes, but the longer you allow it to disturb your thoughts the more extended it is going to linger in your life. Have you ever noticed once one orange mold, then the whole bag is molded? That is the same effect trouble has in our lives. Trouble loves misery, and you have to understand that pain multiplies. If you think more spiritual, live more holy on the spiritual things, then your life will increase better and beautiful things. Now, remember to be patient. Whatever you allow your mind to consume is what's going to release in your life. I always grab me a word of encouragement in my heart. Jesus will spiritually feed your heart and mind while The Holy Spirit will translate it through your soul. I held on to *Proverbs 14:27 "The fear of the Lord is a fountain of life, to depart from the snares of death."* I had to understand that if I can get myself away from the ruins of life, then I could survive much life aggravated assaults, whether it was a sin, people, things or places. The

I can't take one more thing!

snares of life are what always ruin many from receiving a Fountain of Life. I am going to fight for mine, what about you? You must stand and fight for what you believe. I wanted a fountain of hope, life, joy, goodness, miracles, truth, love, good health, blessings, happiness, prosperity, peace, wealth, good times, and so on until I could never let go of that word. I received it with gladness, and it moved into my heart in 1999. Yes, I asked God for a Fountain of Life, full of every need. That word caused me to endeavor deeper, through searching the truth more than any other word in my life. From that moment on, I read that scripture, and it still assures me today. Truly, I find great hope in that word. Even during my weakest times of life, I held on. *Psalm 121:8, "The LORD shall preserve thy going out and thy coming in from this time forth, and even for evermore."*

Now understand I am not perfect though I received that word in 1999 in my living room I had a lot to overcome. Truthfully, not everything could I resist, but the key is that I never quit trying.

I can't take one more thing!

Aggravations are cruel and a regular part of life, you just need to learn to live with them without it removing your joy. The more WISDOM you gain, the fewer life aggravations will appear in your life. Get WISDOM! Don't always be so quick to anger. Also, stop letting simple things upset you. You must grab a form of hope, in a word from God that will stir you up to run for greater. The word will direct you, away from life's aggravations. Anyone and any situation that has a death hold over your life, give it over to Jesus and leave it with Him. He will handle it for you. *Hebrew 11:37, "They were stoned, they were sawn asunder, were tempted, were slain with the sword: they wandered about in sheepskins and goatskins; being destitute, afflicted, tormented;"*

Many cases have proven that many people lose their minds due to something terrible or dramatic that has happened. Sometimes life's loads can put people under a strain of pressure, and not everyone can handle pressure. Nevertheless, that pressure must be released, and not everyone can properly release his or

I can't take one more thing!

her pressures. Then their minds are formed through a chaotic sense, unraveling everything all at once. I have learned to realize some release their forces through engaging in a sin of some form. Whether it be profanity, adultery, drugs, violence, selfishness, stealing and killing. Regardless, it all destroys the person and has victims. Aggravations are powerful; that is why the enemy works so hard to assault our minds. Afterward, many people realize that they have allowed too much to accompany their mind at once. Now the actual attack of the mind begins to take place. Some of our minds are afflicted with material possession, too much gain and too hard to obtain. We are living busy lifestyles and why did we neglect Jesus? Then we think, what is the use? We overfill our lives with bags of bondage that will cause us to become aggravated with our life. However, we are not living in the will of GOD, only living for a man made a god. I know it seems awkward for you to understand this. The majority of the Christians today, are not trying to please GOD. They are trying to reconcile favor from man. If this or that person can be caught up

I can't take one more thing!

by your attention through your material possessions, then yes, they will see that you are about something. If only you can gain this particular individual's attention or particular crowd attention, then you might be noticed, and they will befriend you. Well, the truth of the matter is that God just wants you to become more faithful to Him. Sometimes we allow our unfaithfulness towards God to torment our minds. We should never question Him. He is going to handle our situations regardless of our condition. God wants all of our trust to be firm in Him, being the God over it and in our lives. Regardless of how crazy some things may sound or appear to us, He just wants our faith more in Him. *Psalms 35:9, "And my soul shall be joyful in the Lord: it shall rejoice in His salvation."*

Only God has the actual power to free you from this thing, so stop giving everyone else the opportunity to his or her many babbling words. There are more eyes on you for the wrong reasons than the right reason. It is awkward how God will use little, simple people just to reach you. Once a neighborhood drunk

I can't take one more thing!

inspired me, and I will never forget her, may God rest her soul. That same person God used to encourage me while others laughed was a real blessing to my life. Many people picked on her for being who she was. People that are of little faith cannot get it because they do not understand God in the manner He wants them to. I learned how to rejoice my way through every trial, whether I had to sing, write, shout, cry, pray, or hope in a hopeless situation. I just continued to press my way out. Keep your mind in spiritual shape. Do not let an aggravation interrupt your blessed future. Get the word inside you; it is the only way to increase your faith. Also, let God work that WORD OUT, OF YOU, it will get you fit for what is to come. God is the use of everything that you are going through because it is all to incorporate a dynamic vision for your life. *Job 11:14, (The words of Zophar another friend of Job) "If iniquity is in thine hand, put it far away, and let not wickedness dwell in thy tabernacles."* God is allowing your suffering period, to show people His use and introduce them to your life's purpose. It is not your sufferings that will kill you; it is the wisdom of

I can't take one more thing!

God that will save others. God had to use your sufferings, to show the closest ones around you who He is. I know many looked at me and said, why won't she just sit down and quit? However; they did not understand what Jesus had spoken to me, showed me and promised me. And out of all the hell, I have gone through, I wasn't going to rest until I became more than a conquer! I have had many struggles, aggravated until I questioned Gods ability. But, I was determined to overcome. Your enemies will try to make you look as though you are crazy! However, sometimes you will appear to be crazy as you hold on to your faith. Just keep on, until God prove His word is true and faithful in your life. Do not stop now! Now, if I had given up on God, then you would not be reading this book right now. Quitting and humbling yourself are two different things. However, to many it looked like I was a struggling failure. I had to prove that God was real. I listened to His voice. Suffering for the righteousness only causes you to come out powerful and be more blessed. *Psalm 121:8, "The LORD shall preserve thy going out and thy coming in from this*

I can't take one more thing!

time forth, and even for evermore." For every suffering period in my life, I gained greater faith, greater strength, and greater favor. While I suffered, I learned how to lean more on the word of God. I learned how to be patient with Him. It has caused me to stand and believe greater in the word. It taught me to praise JESUS sincerely, in and out of season. He will be your shelter in the time of a storm. It caused me to mature and develop more spiritually in the gifts that God has given me. I knew when trouble came my way that God was going to be my way maker. *Psalms 136:3 says, "O give thanks to the Lord of lords: for his mercy endureth forever."* God wants you to understand the depth of grace, the things you must suffer through are those very things that are going to build you up. He wants you to know what it means to hold on when you want to let go. Also, God wants you to hang on when you want to give in and to hold on even when you cannot see anything to hold on. I learned though my money looked funny, He had all I need. I held on, and He delivered. I found out through aches and pains that tormented my body no medicine

I can't take one more thing!

was going to help me; God can provide. I gained more than I ever had, just as Job. Nevertheless, if it had not been for my many sufferings, then God would not have had the opportunity to make me who He has made me be. Nevertheless, He is still making me today. Through every aggravated assault on my mind, God had a plan to incorporate me into a blessed and promised life to live in His Divine Favor. He is doing the same thing for you. Because what that old enemy is trying to mean for your evil God is planning it right now for your good. He has a beautiful plan full of unspeakable joy for your future. *Job 32: 20 says, "I will speak, that I may be refreshed: I will open my lips and answer."*

Oh, what is the use? You have a whole lot of you that is needed, wanted and will love to be employed by God. As long as you allow the enemy to surface and use your assaults to aggravate you, then you can never get to the truth of the matter. The subject formed through some equation that only God can find the use as He figures you. I never imagined in

I can't take one more thing!

a million years that God could use me, but He did. Especially being a writer of His Word to Bring Revelation to His People! I am grateful he can use me! I realized that my sufferings were for me to count it all joy. *Psalm 121:8, "The LORD shall preserve thy going out and thy coming in from this time forth, and even for evermore."* Just as our ministry struggled at the times God wanted to spread the ministry in me worldwide; it was through books & music as well as other engagements. It was a revelation and an equation that God used because He had the perfect formula for my life. Nevertheless, I did not know what was going on, and why I was persecuted. After all, I realized it was to get the best to come out of me. However, Jesus had more for me set aside just as he has for you. His purpose for your life will preserve as you go through this! I would have still been a hairstylist and, gossiping and you know all that goes on in a beauty shop. Perhaps, just another co-pastor trying to help the same bunch of people that did not want to be helped or led out of bondage. Jesus' ministry was on the move; He did not let people stop His ministry. You either

I can't take one more thing!

received Him as He was passing by or you didn't. Regardless, Jesus was on a mission to save, and He was on the move to deliver. Now, I understand why. Some people will hold you back, use you, and just won't listen. He too caused my ministry to be on the move. He knew the people I needed to reach. Jesus wants His ministers to be profitable! What is the use? Well, the use of your sufferings is going to be a formula of hope. It is going to be an awaking on the way you use your faith. It will add up to be some form of a miracle; only God will be able to receive the credit. It will formulate a new praise within your heart and produce favor from The Most High to be evident in your life. It will give you a reason to shout because you know the hands of God are upon you. It will produce faith in you that will not be able to sit still. God will be able to speak, and you will be stirred because you would have tasted His sweetness. Job was blessed bountifully by this formula. *Psalm 121:8, "The LORD shall preserve thy going out and thy coming in from this time forth, and even for evermore."* The Lord caused Job's life to was restored

I can't take one more thing!

to a double portion of everything. I can imagine his friends and loved ones marveled at the sight of it, God's replenishing effect on Job's life. God restored Job and multiplied his blessings. Why, because Job never gave up hope on the mighty God He served. For many of years you have allowed man to use you for the wrong reasons, so do not be upset if God wants to use you for all the right reasons. The reason God has chosen you to be employed by Him is simple. He just wanted Satan to recognize that you are His. He had to use you just to show others that you are His, and He is real. He is not willing to share you with anyone. He loves you, and He wants the best for your life. I have never known Jesus to lose any battle, anyone or anything to the forces of the enemy. It is impossible for JESUS to be a failure! So, therefore, right now, count it all joy like never before.

Job 21:6, "Even when I remember I am afraid, and trembling taketh hold on my flesh." When the strongholds of your life are stronger than you, then you need the actual strength you have never known.

I can't take one more thing!

You need the strength of a Shield to protect you from the fiery darts of life. You need a mountain Rock, to cover you when the forces of the enemy are roaring against you and the Oil of your Butter to give you sliding ability. A King that can give you perfect direction, lead you out of the pattern of destruction; also, a Shepherd to look after you when you are headed in harm's way. He is a Judge that will correct you when you are inconceivably wrong; a Refuge that will fight your battle during the times you give up. He has a Fortress of power that you can gain victorious strength, of the highest capacity. An Avenger to avenge your death in the case of a wounded heart and He has the power to demolish any weapon that has formed against you. Our Heavenly Father is a Creator that can speak anything into existence. Miraculous Healer - when the doctors tell you there is nothing that they can do, because He is the Savior of all the earth. A Protector from all hurt, harm, danger, and evil. He is a Provider of sufficiency so that every need in your life will be bountifully met and met on time. A Redeemer to awaken any dead thing within you, so

I can't take one more thing!

that your soul will be granted the Eternal Life promised with pure happiness and peace. He is my Prince of Peace. He is Mercy forever more and full of Grace. Also, Jesus is the truth, always showing me the way towards His marvelous Light.

I can't take one more thing!

Aggravated Assault On Your Mind

"Only the ones that get back up; they will never accept a fall! Show them what you got!"

~ Parice C. Parker

I can't take one more thing!

Aggravated Assault On Your Mind

CHAPTER 3
Endure Your Life Assaults

"Prepare Yourself to Fight And Win!"

~ Parice C. Parker

I can't take one more thing!

CHAPTER 3

Endure Your Life Assaults

Where is everybody? I am in need! During the time you need people, the most are after they have used you! The worst thing I had to get over is how people that claim to love you will get missing when you need them the most. Yes, after they try to destroy every good thing in you, tell them that The Lord has called you. They will act as if you did not hear God right or they will act deaf. Now remember, these are the ones that have claimed to love you. The same people that talk so highly of The Deliverer, but do not think Jesus has enough power to deliver you. Jesus believers they say, but they act as though Jesus has no authority to save! The same Jesus they depend on to

I can't take one more thing!

take care all of their needs is the same Jesus that has the power to call anyone He pleases into the ministry. Many will begin to run as far away as they can, just to get away from you. I guess they do not believe Jesus has enough power to cleanse the ones He calls. It's about as backward as it gets. Yeah, when I was in the world, having parties and giving free drinks, everybody was there. We always ran out of room, food and drinks. Still now, if I cook a meal today, they all will tend to show up and guess what, without an invitation. However, the church is out of the question. I still cannot figure that one out. These are the kind of people you do not need in your life. They are users and abusers. I had to realize that when I was facing death. One thing I can say about God, if He uses you, it will all be well worth it. However, man cannot give you near what God can. If you cannot be there for me in the time of need, then why take up space in my life? I am not Jesus, neither am I not planning to miss my opportunity to eternal life, simply because of cold hearts. You are good for everything to them, but not worthy enough to call on Jesus. Um, think about that.

I can't take one more thing!

Now these are the same ones you see on Sunday sitting in church, saying amen and shouting as they jump over the pews. Especially, when the pastor says, "Jesus has all power!" I just had to throw this in, because I believe in The Power of Jesus, the Power of His name (Jesus), The Power of Prayer and undoubtedly The Power of Faith. Family and friends should support their loved ones in ministry. For the simple fact, they should want their family to saved too. Truly, God is love, and many need to act more in it. "Understand, my family, supported me well in ministry, and they still do." Help your family run the race, assist them to reach heaven. God will bless you more. I always teach my children to stick together. Once they grow up, I know at least one will follow after the minister and us. I am teaching my children that no matter what, they should support one another whole hardily. Especially when they are trying to live for the Lord. One needs all the help they can get. Being a minister is powerful. A spiritual leader must fight off more demons than anyone, which is why the family is so important to support. Stop looking at the

I can't take one more thing!

individual in your family that is called to minister and help them fight the good fight of faith. The enemy is purposed to destroy them. If you saw your brother or sister being jumped and robbed by others, would you sit there and help ridicule them, or would you help them out? It is that simple with a ministry. I see so many fallen pastors and wounded spiritual leaders destroyed, all because no one would assist them to fight the enemies off. They were jumped and could not withstand the fight. Imagine if it were you called, wouldn't you want your family's support too? I've seen a lot of support in many ministries, and still not satisfied. Remember, ministry starts at home and we all should help our own first instead of standing in judgment. I just believe a family that prays together stays together. There is more power in unity prayer than secular prayer. I teach my children to stick together because Jesus has all the power. How would I look trying to help, love, and save a bunch a people and do not care about my own? Is that pleasing unto God? Wake Up! God Can Use Any Body, At Any Time. Always support your own, pray for them and

I can't take one more thing!

believe that JESUS is All Powerful. I have learned to appreciate anyone still running the race of ministry; it is extremely challenging and yes, the strong will survive. I pray deeply for those that are in the ministry, to continue. We all need prayer. All Pastors need sincere hearts praying for them. Pray for every pastor you see, for the Body of Christ has been under attack. Many say they believe, now is the time to act like it. Believers, Wake Up! Stop the Masquerade Ball and wake up! God is love.

When your life assaults appear, destruction begins to follow. The wind of assaults will flourish in your life as a rose bush, but it will not be a beautiful sight. Anger will arise afflicting your mind. *Job 31:23, "For destruction from God was terror to me, and because of his highness I could not endure."* Job once had his life in full order, it was a beautiful life, and he did not need anything. He had what most could only dream of, and he accumulated substance in abundance. He had wealth, good family, riches, land and favor from everyone (though he thought). We all know those are the ones that are nowhere to be found

I can't take one more thing!

when you are in need! Many looked up to him as being prestigious, well to do man and appeared to be a role model. His life was planned to the, and his accomplishments were award winning. This man had conquered life overflowing with greatness. However, one day his perfect life to many was terribly destroyed. The storms began to rise, and the winds shattered Job's luxurious lifestyle. His relationships with many begin to demolish. His family was consumed, and things disappeared right before his eyes. He has started to feel the terrible pains of life. His strength was weakening, as his body grew faint. Sickness began to take over, but Job held on. Devastation hit every part of his life, in a terrible way. Surely, you can relate to some of his turmoil and feel the beating of the forceful winds pounding his life away. It could not have been me. God will put no more on us than we can bear. Nevertheless, I know the enemy was feasting on his destruction period. He enjoyed every terrible thing that happened to Job. It is a hard thing to hold on to something you cannot grip, to keep your faith when things in your life are twirling in chaos. It is more

I can't take one more thing!

difficult to hope when all else fails in your life. When terrible things begin to happen for no reason, and you did not see it coming. Affliction will cause you excruciating pain as the storms hit your life in full devastation. Job was crying out to God as though He has turned a death ear.

Job 1:1, "There was a man in the land of UZ, whose name was Job; and that man was perfect, and one that feared God, and eschewed evil."

In most cases there does not always have to be a cause, which you did something wrong. Sometimes God wants to test you, as the enemy wants to dismember your trust in God. He does not wish you to believe God exist. If He can destroy your life with many different terrible things, then perhaps your faith will cease too. That is why he pounds so forcefully trying to tear your faith down. He wants it to wash away in the storm. Truly, that is the enemy's objective. To destroy your faith. Once your faith consumed, then you are destroyed! The enemy also has a plan for your life, and that is to destroy it. The more He can allow

I can't take one more thing!

you to feel the many life assaults, he can afflict your faith walk. It angers Him when we succeed in life as we overcome devastation. The enemy wants God destroyed in you. The thing that has assaulted your mind was sent for the purpose to tear you down, but you have to grow stronger no matter what comes your way. It is either going to be a winning mark for one or the other. Prove to the world who you serve. The enemy or your Heavenly Father? Whose side are you own? You can either give in to the enemy or become an overcomer.

It is a hurting thing when you are trying your best to do what is right, and everything is going wrong. However, it hurts more when people do not help you and see you suffering. More than that, especially when they profess JESUS is LORD, and they are family. I went through a rough period in my life. I lost everything. Yes, times grow hard in the life of a first family too. All those so-called people, nowhere to be found unless they were trying to stir up trouble. I thought how I had opened my doors and treated them as my own for years. As I loved them,

I can't take one more thing!

they did not return that kind of love when I needed it the most. You understand, I am confident you can feel the pain. I took from my children plenty of times, just to help others. However, not one asked the question - if they could assist in any way? They wanted to criticize us when our life was going through the storm, and they did not care if my children had a hot meal or a roof over their head. However, they wanted to know what was going wrong in our life. People will scorn you when you just simply need them to gather and pray. When you see trouble in someone's life, do not make it worst. Contribute to making it better! Show them, LOVE, because one day it could be you! If I did not earnestly know The Holy Spirit, I would have surely died. However, a portion of me did, and that part is not willing to be raised from the dead. Now, I am only willing to be used by JESUS. He Helped Me! *Job 1:2,* "And there were born unto him seven sons and three daughters." Evidently, Job needed his children; he endured sufferings that many could not handle without losing their mind. Our children bring hope to us in a day of sorrow, laughter during a time as

I can't take one more thing!

we are in tears. I can imagine the were the sparkle in his eyes. One day they all died at once. That tore him up in grief, but he still had to trust God. He knew no other way. *Job 1:3, "His substance also was seven thousand sheep, and three thousand camels, and five hundred yoke of oxen, and five hundred she asses, and a very great household; so that this man was the greatest of all the men of the east."*

His worth was huge, and he had accumulated great wealth. The LORD had blessed him dearly, and he gained plentifully. Nevertheless, one day He lost all of his substance, and He still trusted God. How many of us can trust God during a time of great lost? Sometimes we will be tried in that manner. I know, I was. We must thank God for our worst conditions, for in all things we should bless His name. We do not understand nature and the many destructive things that it will bring forth. However, even through your most aggravated life assaults you need to know that Jesus is working on your behalf. Know that He is your Savior! Still, we must be thankful for it all. It is a hard thing thanking God for losing your substance. Moreover,

I can't take one more thing!

even greater trusting God after your children have past. Ask yourself the question. Do I thank God for my worst living conditions? Do I glorify Him, while I am living through the storms? *1 Thessalonian 5:18, "In everything give thanks: for this is the will of God in Christ Jesus concerning you."* The greatest glory you can give to our Heavenly Father is thanking Him during your worst times. It is because you should be able to count on Him for anything. When I go through a storm, I have learned to go through with my praise. If I don't know anything else, I know that Jesus has everything I need and some more. *1 Thessalonian 5:18, "In everything give thanks: for this is the will of God in Christ Jesus concerning you."* I learned to thank Him no matter what comes or what goes, and as I thanked Him, I praised Him with gladness. I begin to count my troubles for joy. There is no way Jesus will allow me to go through and not have the power to bring me out. I have learned to glorify Him while I am going through knowing that trouble doesn't last always. God loves you through it all, and He would not allow you to bear something you could not handle.

I can't take one more thing!

Job was a good man with noble qualities and had proved greatly to God that he was true and faithful. However, the enemy was allowed to bring forth much destruction to His life. No matter what you are going through and must go through, you have to stand. Things are going to appear evil in your life, but you have to stand. Your strength is going to weaken as you go through, but you have to hold on. Tears are going to fall from your cheeks, and the punches may grow stronger as it forces into your gut, but you have to get back up. However, even though you lay awake and cry all night long, you must hold on. You must hold on to Him during the worst times of your life because it is life threatening. Never let Him go! No matter what you lose, what or who dies, how much affliction appears in your life at one time. Hold on to God.

Job 1:6, "Now there was a day when the sons of God came to present themselves before the LORD, and Satan came among them." Though the winds shuffle, the assaults get stronger, and irritations grow wilderness. Still hold on to your faith. Never let JESUS go and never dismiss Him from your life. It's

I can't take one more thing!

the time that He will begin to work wonders. When you want to give up, just give in. When your arms cannot be lifted, praise His name with your voice. During the terrible times, you cannot speak, meditate on His Word. Because anytime affliction comes into your life, God will be standing right beside you taking control of your terrible times. It is the most valuable time of your spiritual development. Do not let your mind circle in on your afflictions, but allow it to hold on to God's mercy. He will have mercy on you at the time of your need. As long as you can remain faithful to God and believe Him to be your deliverer, that is enough to cause God to work beyond measure in your life. Where you cannot reach, God can. His arms have no limits. He is a merciful God, and His mercy endures forever, with no ending point. *Job 1:7, "And the LORD said unto Satan, Whence comest thou?* Then Satan answered the Lord, and said, From going to and fro in the earth, and from walking up and down in it." God had truly blessed Job and Job had proved himself greatly to God. However, there was something too good about Job that Satan noticed. He saw how

I can't take one more thing!

blessed Job was, and Satan wanted his blessings. You often wonder why me? Well just as Job, Satan wants your blessings. He loves stealing from others especially those that possess great qualities in God. Satan cannot get the attention He wants from God or the blessings you have received. So, therefore, He wishes to steal yours. It is your life that Satan wished he had. These assaults are not intended to kill you; it would be too easy. Satan wants to destroy you slowly. He wants you to suffer because you believe in God. It is all a test. While Satan is trying one end, God is testing you on the other. Which test are you going to pass? Suffering from the enemy or suffering for the Righteous? God can only supply mercy to the ones that need Him and call on Him. *Psalms 136:1, "O give thanks unto the LORD; for he is good; for his mercy endureth forever."*

    Job always had everything he needed. He had so much until he gave much of it away to others that were in need. God replenishes us through His mercy. Job knew that there were no limits on God's mercy, His mercy endures forever! Even when we are

I can't take one more thing!

satisfied with what we have, God always has a way of replenishing us with more. Job had the experience of being blessed with more than enough, because of mercy. Mercy is for those that are in terrible shape, messed up living situations during terrible times and simply are in the need of a miracle. The job was always blessed. He lived an upright life, and he was the perfect candidate for God to prove to Satan that He was faithful. God knows how much you can bear. He knew He could depend on Job to make Him appear to be worthy. God spreads Himself, because of faith. He is created in us by our hope, and He is published to many through our faith. Faith is what identifies God. You need belief to make your life speak that God is your Alpha & Omega. Only meaning He is your life beginner, everything in between and for eternity. He wants you to introduce Him to Satan as your God through your faith. Though you need Him to work wonders right now, that is the same manner in which He needs you to have greater confidence. Believe in Him that He is and for you, He will. *Job 1:8, "In addition, the LORD said unto Satan, Hast thou*

I can't take one more thing!

considered my servant Job, which there is none like him in the earth, a perfect and an upright man, one that feareth God, and eschewed evil?" Satan has no power unless God gives him permission. Everything that has happened in your life was directed from Heaven. Nothing with any power can move in your life unless God approves of it first. God gave this approval to Satan to have His way in Job's life, but no power to take his life. All I can say is that the more destruction that comes in your life is, the greater you will be blessed if you hold onto God. Just as it was a beginning time for your troubles, it will soon be an ending. Hold onto God and keep your faith, it will soon be over. You wonder why you were assaulted, well God wanted to show up to you as a trophy. Show everyone that your faith in Christ is award winning.

Job 1:9, Then Satan answered the LORD, and said, "Doth Job fear God for naught?" God does not intend you to be afraid during troubling times, but He does expect you to claim Him greater to be your God. Focus on God, focus on safety and focus on your faith. God is not the God of fear, but the God of Heavenly

I can't take one more thing!

Rewards. Once you focus on what kind of faith you have, then things will appear differently in your life. We all at one time or another have some faith, but is it the faith God want you to have? Is your faith sufficient or does it need to grow larger? Is it more in you, your materials, job or someone else? There is only one faith that moves the hand of God, and it is TRUST! You must TRUST In HIM!

I know during a terrible storm in my life when it seemed though trouble was all around. I had a few that I least expected to come forth to bless my family. Often He will use strangers to bless you. Most of them did not go to church, but they took the time to love. I do understand how Job felt when the very people he had been there for were looking down on him. They did not see him do wrong, they just assumed he wasn't as righteous as he appeared. That is how I felt as my storms were raging, but I still held on. God has a mighty way of increasing our faith, and He will cause your faith to trust Him more. As you go through this, your faith will be inflated. He is waiting for you to need Him more and more. He wants to grow larger in

I can't take one more thing!

you. Sometimes we think we have all we need and in most cases, we do not. Realize the impact of your afflictions, they are ALL POWERFUL! Affliction only strengthens and builds you to become more faithful, and expands your trust in HIM. It awards God, as we grow to trust Him. I thought I had faith. As I grew in the word, I did. When things in my life begin to twirl, I realized if I was going to get through this, then I needed some strength I never had. God continued to increase me with greater faith. The more major trouble you bear, the greater your faith will have to be enlarged. *Psalms 1:2, "O give thanks to the LORD of lords: for His mercy endureth forever."*

God always has mercy on us, and He is everlasting *(Psalms 136)*. He has enough for every prisoner and for every sinner that calls on Him at once. You cannot limit mercy and mercy is for all that believe in Him. Mercy has no depth, no love conditions, no respect for a person or situation and no limits. It does not matter who you are, what you have done or how worthy you are; mercy is for all. God is plenteous in it. Moreover, it is available right now to

I can't take one more thing!

all that need mercy. Mercy delivered the sick, caused the dead to rise, woke you up this morning and took the crack pipe out of a mother's hands. Mercy will go in the worst places, and supply a need. Mercy is not afraid to go into the most dangerous places, conditions, or circumstances just to deliver people. It has caused sinners to become righteous, saved many from the pits of hell and made many receive the gift of love. Give thanks to God, because He is God over our lives and full of mercy. No matter where you are, how troubled your life is or how much you need, God will supply you with grace. Job knew trouble greater than anyone (other than Jesus) in the Bible and experienced more affliction than many. He was tormented in every area of his life, but He still held on. However, the pain will bring forth bruises while your wounds will bring forth healing power. Satan cannot understand mercy because He is too busy working on it.

Remember Satan is jealous of you and he wants what you have. He wishes he had the opportunity to the tree of life, but he can never receive it. So, therefore, he wishes to ruin your chance. He wants the

I can't take one more thing!

God in you to be destroyed! *Job 1:10, "Hast not thou made an hedge about him, and about his house, and about all that he hath on every side?* Thou hast blessed the work of his hands, and his substance is increased in the land." It does not matter your gain, wealth, health or degree of life. Satan wants it all. Though some things in your life are priceless to lose, with it comes to a reward. Though Job's children died, he still had the opportunity of knowing them one time or another. He still had the memories of them being in his life and nothing can take the place of memories. I know you cannot understand why some things happen, but some people never had the experience of even baring children. Once you bare things in your life that are priceless, you have an opportunity to appreciate the greater. Many couples have struggled a lifetime trying to bare children and could not. Some only have just a moment to share a small part of their lives with their children, such as Job. We do not have all the explanations, but knowing we must go on with our lives depending fully on mercy to carry us through times as these. In all things, we must be thankful and

I can't take one more thing!

pray that mercy will appear. No matter how our lives have begun and no matter what enters, afterward, we all need to hold onto God. Though life is strenuous and trouble grows, we still have someone that needs us to survive, and they expect mercy to carry us through it all. Mercy has a way of comforting you when you do not want to live. Just when you give up, the Love of MERCY will appear to cause you to want a fresh breath and desire a new start. Mercy has a way of causing you to want to survive. *Job 1:11, "But put forth thine hand now, and touch all that he hath, and he will curse thee to thy face."* Satan's objective for your life is to make you go against God. I know times as I suffered, I tried all I had to live right, and it angered me to feel the pressures of life. Satan wants you to turn back, and he does not want you to grow any more in faith. He wants to anger your life, and he will use anyone that he can, to upset you and make you go against God. Remember God is depending on you during your worst trials of life to exalt Him higher. Nevertheless, Satan wants you to dismember JESUS out of your life. As your troubles grow worst,

I can't take one more thing!

the enemy wants you to hate God. Satan tries all he has to pull the worst out of us, and he just does not believe in anything good. When you are assaulted, you must learn self-control and be patient with God. Sometimes aggravations can make us say things we should not. *(I Peter 2: 11 & 12) "It can make us do things we ought not and treat people how we should not."* If you get in a tough place in life, it can either make you or break you. Satan wants to break you. You must sustain affliction with joy from on high, no matter how hard it hurts. Depend on mercy to deliver you. It does not matter where the disorder occurs within your life. Just depend solely on mercy. We have to control our language even when you want to curse. We have to act in a manner of calmness when aggravations grow at its worst. *Proverbs 15:1, "A SOFT answer turneth away wrath: but grievous words stir up anger."* We cannot allow Satan to make us curse our God because He depends on you. He knew He could depend on Job to handle himself in a proper manner. He proved to Satan that he was a prominent man of high integrity. God also wants to depend on

I can't take one more thing!

you too. *Job 1:12 says, "And the LORD said unto Satan, Behold, all that he hath is in thy power, only upon himself put not forth thine hand."* Therefore, Satan went forth from the presence of the LORD. When everything in your life is destroyed, God is not going to allow you to be consumed. The wrath is only around you, but God is in the midst of it. Though it takes away people you love, things you have worked hard for, and afflicted your body, God will not let it kill you. We have to trust Him. Wait with an expectation for God to have mercy on you, just as Job *(Palms 136)*. Regardless of how little or how large your faith has proved itself, there is still more room for your faith to be enlarged. It depends on your life preservation point of how much faith you will need. God wants us to have faith far bigger than a mustard seed. Your mustard seed faith is just your beginning stage. My faith had to grow because Jesus knew what my future possessed. He could not increase my territory without increasing my confidence. God was sizing up my faith to match my future, just as He is doing for you. Faith is increased more through every

I can't take one more thing!

life affliction. Especially, through the assaults that only Jesus could help us out! *Thessalonians 1:6 says, "And ye became followers of us, and of the Lord, having received the word in much affliction, with joy of the Holy Ghost:"*

Job knew God in a manner that many did not. He was aware that God in The Spirit and In Truth! There are plenty areas of our lives that we know God, but the truth is in the word. Job was one that spent quality time in receiving life instructions through the word. So, therefore, when times got hard, and he could not endure, The Holy Ghost stepped in spiritually. God will not let you fall during your troubling times. Though the pressures of life weigh you down, God will lift you up. He will be the lifter up of your head. *(Psalms 3:3) He only wants us to endure as much as we can because endurance will strengthen you.* It's preparing you for greater. For every mind aggravation, His word will deliver us on time. When you are going through troubling times, then JESUS must produce His WORD to come forth in your life. When you cannot hold on any longer, because of your afflictions, then

I can't take one more thing!

The WORD will hold on for you. When you are afflicted and cannot live anymore, then The WORD will live through you. The WORD gives life and life brings forth joy. As The Holy Ghost ushers the enemy out of your presence. Even Satan knew how to act in the presence of The Lord. He could not touch anything around Job until he was out of the presence of The Lord. Nothing ungodly can exist in the presence of The Holy Ghost. *Job 21:6, "Even when I remember I am afraid and trembling taketh hold on my flesh."* No matter what appears in your life, know that The WORD will not fail you. Just present your situation with The WORD and watch it prevail powerfully in your life. As you speak to your circumstance with The WORD, power will unfold, and your situation will begin to change. The WORD gives life so remember when God speaks; it is over. The best way to get rid of Satan is through the presence of The Holy Ghost. Speak the word, until you are delivered!

Job 21:6, "Even when I remember I am afraid, and trembling taketh hold on my flesh." When the strongholds of your life are stronger than you, then

I can't take one more thing!

you need the actual strength you have never known. You need the strength of a Shield to protect you from the fiery darts of life. You need a mountain Rock, to cover you when the forces of the enemy are roaring against you and the Oil of your Butter to give you sliding ability. A King that can give you precise direction, lead you out of the pattern of destruction; also, a Shepherd to look after you when you are headed in harm's way. He is a Judge that will correct you when you are inconceivably wrong; a Refuge that will fight your battle during the times you give up. He has a Fortress of power that you can gain victorious strength, of the highest capacity. An Avenger to avenge your death in the case of a wounded heart and He has the power to demolish any weapon that has formed against you. Our Heavenly Father is a Creator that can speak anything into existence. Miraculous Healer - when the doctors tell you there is nothing that they can do, because He is the Savior of all the earth. A Protector from all hurt, harm, danger, and evil. He is a Provider of sufficiency so that every need in your life will be bountifully met and met on time. A

I can't take one more thing!

Redeemer to awaken any dead thing within you, so that your soul will be granted the Eternal Life promised with pure happiness and peace. He is my Prince of Peace. He is Mercy forever more and full of Grace. Also, Jesus is the truth, always showing me the way towards His marvelous Light.

I can't take one more thing!

Aggravated Assault On Your Mind

"Power, plus power equals more power. What are your associates adding to your life? Sum it up!"

~Parice C. Parker

I can't take one more thing!

Aggravated Assault On Your Mind

CHAPTER 4
What Are You Feeding Your Mind

"What Goes In, Must Come Out!"

~ Parice C. Parker

I can't take one more thing!

CHAPTER 4

What Are You Feeding Your Mind?

Imagine for a moment how you have been influenced in the past, by putting your trust into the very person you loved. You showed them, deep love, as you loved them dearly. The direction you have allowed them to take you has caused you distractions. You must find your way back to your goals. We tend to give certain people power over our destiny without realizing it, such as friends, family, and especially those unexpected love triangles we all have seemed to get caught in at one time or another. We just only stray away from our goals, and we stop focusing on them. Under any circumstances, put your trust in the people. *(Matthew 27:43) Influence of the mind is a directional*

I can't take one more thing!

pattern for your life's destination point whether it is good or bad. The decisions you make and the direction you will take can lead you to destruction or an abundance of happiness for a real. Presumably, you have made some wrong choices. Indeed, we have all socialized in the wrong environment and agreed to the wrong people or things. Besides, sometimes God will only allow us in someone's life just for a season. Now, if you want to move into the better things that life has to offer, it is time to put on your thinking cap. Speculate who and what you agreeing with. You must consider your entire surroundings and realize what is being produced in your life. There is no question in the matter. You must not tolerate being used or being irresponsible. Do not neglect any of your situations for what they are. Look at your life and the people you have chosen to be a part of. Undoubtedly, who they are shall eventually identify who you are. Notice what is being added to your life, because of them. Perhaps, even what they have caused you to become! Believe who you associate with because soon you will walk in full agreement.

I can't take one more thing!

Trusting in GOD and letting HIM be your guide will build your daily confidence. He will give you strength as well as security. *Job 33:4 says, "The Spirit of God hath made me, and the breadth of the Almighty hath given me life."* Prove your love to HIM daily through feeding your mind knowledge of the WORD. Allow yourself to be enhanced through your learning ability, by studying just a few minutes a day. Spend quality time with The WORD and it will add greatness to your life. Your life will be impacted by power, as you will also receive great revelation. This will re-adjust your mind to be able to receive instruction from the Holy Spirit. You know that God is your Maker, the one that will feed your life every second of the day, and the one that causes The Spirit of Righteousness to live in you. You will grow into a spiritual trust in Him, regardless of what comes your way. No one or thing will be able to break your spiritual bond with Jesus, once you become a believer. *Romans 8:35, "Who shall separate us from the love of Christ? Shall tribulation, or distress, or persecution, or famine, or nakedness, or peril, or the sword*

I can't take one more thing!

separate you?" This knot will stay tied because my life depends on it. Life aggravations are designed to disconnect us from The Holy Spirit. The enemy's objective is to disrupt your vision, mess up your plan and to stop your Appointment with your Divine Destiny! God longs for us trust in Him through our daily meditation in the word. Our greatest deception is to stop believing The WORD, which is why the enemy tries so hard to remove you away from it. The enemies will put in overtime to ruin your life and destroy you. *Mark 4:15, "And these are they by the wayside, where the word is sown; but when they have heard the word, Satan cometh immediately, and taketh away the word that was sown into their hearts."* Now it is time for you to put in overtime with WORD INSTRUCTION! The more you trust Jesus, the more confident you will become. Our eyes may see one thing, but God wants us to know all things through Him. The same way Satan comes to destroy The WORD out of you, you need to be fighting to destroy the hell out of your life. The WORD of God is like a well of life, and Satan does not intend for you to dwell on the good things

I can't take one more thing!

that The WORD will offer. What may appear before your eyes are not what appears in God's eyesight? Satan knows that the WORD possesses great power, and he does not want you to have it. *Psalms 119:148, "Mine eyes prevent the night watches, that I might meditate in thy word."* I have seen many people lose wonderful life opportunities because they did not meditate on the word. God wants you to meditate on His goodness, His might, and His Word. *1 Corinthians 2:9, "But as it is written, EYE HATH NOT SEEN, NOR EAR HEARD, NEITHER HAVE ENTERED INTO THE HEART OF MAN, THE THINGS WHICH GOD HATH PREPARED FOR THEM THAT LOVE HIM."* If we as people of righteousness allowed the Word to enter truly into our hearts, this world would be just like heaven! Because we would be All Powerful, if we would just let His Word come into our hearts. Satan does not want that. He comes immediately to steal the Word out of our hearts. Satan destroys peoples' faith because he took the Word. After all that, the ones without the Word begin to perish. However, if many would fight to keep

I can't take one more thing!

their WORD, new life will come. Personally, I could not have survived, if it wasn't for the Word. Many days I did not feel like going to church, but I pushed my way as though my life depended on it. I needed The Word! I had to go to a church where I know the pastor preached and taught a powerful Word. Why, because my life depended on it. Satan had such an attack on my life; I had to run continuously to the WORD. The same manner the enemies had assaulted me, I begin to allow the WORD to attack them back. I realized that if I was going to become more than a conqueror, then I needed Christ to strengthen me. Only the WORD can defend you against Satan. When you are ready to overcome truly anything in your life, then you will do all that is necessary to achieve like never before. Satan knows who I am, and that is why his attacks were so mighty in my life. Now the key is that once you realize who you are in Christ Jesus, then you will get up and fight. If Satan and his crew can put in overtime to ruin your life, then you need to be putting in double time with the WORD, to get Satan out of your life. Only the WORD can defeat Satan!

I can't take one more thing!

Only the WORD! God has a word of encouragement for everything we go through in life. There is a WORD to prepare us for life's obstacles, a Word to strengthen us before we go through, and a Word to bring us out. In His word, you will be strengthened, and you will gain courage. However, our eyes see what they want. God wants us to see Him through His many possibilities and His WORD. *Romans 8:35, "Who shall separate us from the love of Christ? Shall tribulation, or distress, or persecution, or famine, or nakedness, or peril, or sword?"* God wants to show you the pleasures of faith in Him. He does not expect things in our life to cause us to be without anything. Yes, some things are very challenging and hard to overcome. However, you can overcome! He wants to make all your heart's desires not just possible, but He wants them in your life. Nevertheless, your SPIRITUAL EYES want you to believe in the impossible. The enemy wants you to see the wrong things and does not wish you to be a partaker in anything that is going to make you happy. Again, that is why the enemy attempts to harm you through

I can't take one more thing!

tribulations, distress, sickness, sin and so on. Just don't give up. *Job 23:14, "For he appointed the things that are appointed for me: and many such things are with him."* God knows what you are going to have to go through to be pruned towards perfection. In many cases, our afflictions are to strengthen us. These assaults on our lives are to awaken us, as well as sharpen our character and to build our patience. Job was one that patiently waited on The LORD. He knew His Maker would rescue him from tormenting hell. Not all that Job experienced was easy. However, he still waited on The LORD. Through his sadness, tears, distress, spiritual reflection, hurt, depression, sourness, and misery – he patiently waited! There is absolutely nothing that has or will ever happen to you that God does not know. So, therefore, just be patient with The LORD. *Romans 8:35, "Who shall separate us from the love of Christ? Shall tribulation, or distress, or persecution, or famine, or nakedness, or peril, or sword?"* Surely, if Job survived his many aggravated assaults at once, then so can you. Job was tried in every kind of way by the enemy, but Satan could not

I can't take one more thing!

separate Job from the love of Christ. No matter how Satan tried, Job passed his test. God was preparing Job with great patience.

As we meditate on His goodness, God can begin to perform a spiritual work in our hearts, mind, body and soul by controlling our mind with the word. The correct word brings forth wisdom and knowledge bring forth truth as truth sets us free. Designate your study time by planning it into your daily activities. Putting it on your things to do list, and make it a priority. Just as you send your children to school during the weekday mornings and expect them to be more educated. You too, as a need adult time set aside daily for spiritual development. Empower your mind by feeding it so that you can receive a better understanding of how to live and maintain a more productive life. We encounter so many different spirits in a day and remember spirits are transferable. If you are not in the WORD, some of the wicked spirits can begin to possess your life. Many do not realize it until their lives are almost ruined. The Spirit knows the Spirit by the Spirit. The key is which spirits are you

I can't take one more thing!

entangling on a daily basis? So, therefore, if you want God to lead your day, daily meditation is a must. Each day you meditate on JESUS, He will cause you to grow stronger in the Word. The most important part of your study is receiving an understanding of what GOD has for you. Let the WORD enter your heart, as you meditate. Your life purpose should be a production of your faith. What is your faith producing? The word of God needs to soak into your heart until it saturates your mind with power to defeat anyone, anything, and any assault. *Luke 24:49, "And, behold, I send the promise of my Father upon you: but tarry ye in the city of Jerusalem, until ye be endued with power from on high."* Jesus wanted us to be comforted by His WORD. Only His WORD can cover you in a true time of need. No, things in life will not always go as we want them. However, stay covered with The Blood while things are not as you desire. During stressful times, the enemy can play dangerously with your mind. He interferes with our righteousness through people, things, hard times, and when we make bad decisions, he loves it. When our lives appear as

I can't take one more thing!

Romans 8:35 that is when he tempts us the more. He wants to separate us from the love of Christ. Satan knows when and how to enter in your life. That is why he is The Master Thief! His purpose is to steal your happiness, and disturb our good homes until he separates us from JESUS! Often people are aggravated only because they have allowed Satan to enter during a terrible time in their life. He entered when you were not tarrying in THE WORD. Your wait may not come when you want, but continue to wait for the WORD. Wait, until you are delivered. Many have welcomed Satan in and did not realize they were playing with fire. He brought more enemies with him, than most can handle! Satan will trick many, and often he also enters through the WORD, being helpful and kind.

He has truly deceived many, with his eye-catching treats. Things we think we are strong enough to handle, and it is not so. Once God delivers you from something, never go back. I once knew these people they loved to entertain. They were good people, not causing or meaning anyone harm. They just loved partying and had fun. However, one day of fun

I can't take one more thing!

ultimately scorned their lives forever. One party too much has caused them to lose everything. We must be careful even when we entertain. Make sure all your entertainment is clean and give no room for the enemy to sneak in.

Someone else will introduce a new God to the ones that are weak, due to a life crisis. Perhaps, they could be the smart and faithful ones of the family to cause others to follow quickly after the new faith. Stay covered in JESUS name, it is power in the name of JESUS you should not separate from! Once you grow stronger in the Word, through the Spirit of Jesus things will not be able to hurt you anymore.

Other times we go through things that we should not have to deal with. An example, a cheating spouse. The one you dearly love, but still contributed great family abuse by neglecting their marriage vows. Everyone else's love ones, but yours! I consider it family abuse and it is sickening. The children notice tension in the home and they too are often affected. Just as you feel the hurt, they too are tormented. Yes,

I can't take one more thing!

it is aggravating, and I simply say some things you just do not have to live in. Get clearance with our Heavenly Father first, before making any drastic decisions. When the aggravations are possible for you to get rid of instead of ignoring their faults, then get rid of it. The worst kind of aggravation to deal with is the one that you should depend on loving you. However, they assault you in more ways than one. After all, your children are counting on you for a better tomorrow. So, therefore, we should rely on the Word of GOD TO DIRECT OUR PATH TODAY. Have you ever gone to JESUS and He began to assault you? No, because love will always love you back. However, your trial will make you think otherwise. Stop taking the abuse. Know what direction your life is going in, and be prepared to become more than a conqueror as you are delivered.

Surely, my marriage has not been the best marriage, but we tried as much as we could. I stayed angry than loving at times. Plenty of times I wanted it to be over. What if I would have left my husband within the first five years? I would not have our first

I can't take one more thing!

two children before we had lost four. We tried to have a baby but was not successful. The doctors said, "I could not have children." Perhaps, if I would have divorced my husband within the first eight years, you would not have the opportunity of reading this book. This book originated out of me feeling the aggravated assaults of life. One night I was so angry at him and life, I wanted to do something crazy. I was led by The Spirit of Righteousness to write out my anger, instead of doing something I would regret. I did, and it became the introduction of Aggravated Assault on Your Mind! God always has a mighty way of turning a bad situation around. Often people walk out on their prosperity because they do not have the patience to wait. Many do not have what it takes to endure. I know I would not be an author if I had left my husband. Though many things I disagreed with, we worked it out. I also was no sweet thing to him all the time. We both have had our in-differences, but we hung in there. Being impatience will cause your destiny to be forfeited. Never take things into your consideration. Always seek The Almighty's approval

I can't take one more thing!

first. Many times I wanted to leave, but after praying about it, He always told me to stay. To many I looked like a fool, but those people were not my God, and I did not listen to them. It is something how so many people trust the judgment of others, before The Judgment of Jesus! I did not understand all that I was going through, but through it all, He was making me. I grew diligently in patience; it is something valuable you will need to succeed. Patience is a necessity for development. Without patience, you will not get far in life. Although with patience, there are no limits. The key to life assaults is to hang in there. But, while you are hanging, do something that you have never done. It will take something new to get rid of something old. The change starts from within first. As I wrote many books, my change started in me first. I stopped trying to change him and begin becoming a living example. No matter what you are going through, if there is a Most High, there is a possibility for a change! As long as there is a possibility, then it is already done in JESUS name!

I can't take one more thing!

Knowledge brings forth understanding and understanding helps you to gain WISDOM. Job was one that had WISDOM. He was able to endure great affliction because he had WISDOM. *Romans 8:35 says, "Who shall separate us from the love of Christ? Shall tribulation, or distress, or persecution, or famine, or nakedness, or peril, or sword?"* Once you have WISDOM, the enemy cannot fool you. We all need spiritual development, and no one should just wait on Sunday morning to receive it. Many have wondered why they are not growing, developing and being enriched when they appear in church. It is all because they did not feed their mind spiritually before they entered. Job spiritually fed his mind before he began his terrible life assaults. He knew The WORD! *Luke 24:49, "And, behold, I send the promise of my Father upon you: but tarry ye in the city of Jerusalem, until ye be endued with power from on high."* Therefore, when things got rough, Job was still able to hold on. You must know your word when things go wrong in life. The word is your weapon. How can one fight a good fight without a defense? The WORD will

I can't take one more thing!

defend you when you are about to lose your mind. The WORD will decide on your next move when the enemy figures he has you trapped in an unmovable situation. The WORD will guide you into a place of peace. When the hell is breaking loose in your life, the Word will usher it out. The WORD will love you when everyone else will walk with you. When the enemy thinks he has you cornered, The WORD will cause you to begin to move. Stay connected to the WORD, until you be endued with power from on high in your hell storm. Only the WORD can comfort you when you are in the worst shape of your life. Believe me, I know, and so does Job. The WORD will also heal you when there is no cure. Make sure you have the WORD to keep you covered.

Psalms 8:6, "Thou madest him to have dominion over the works of thy hands; thou hast put all things under his feet:" You must know your maker. Meditating on His word will cause you to triumph through any life assault because you will know that He has the power to make it all happen. Do not let people or things upset you to the point that you

I can't take one more thing!

do not want to live a normal and healthy life. I once heard someone say; "I have been hurt so many times," when others continue to abuse your love, leave them alone. I do not want a husband. Understand the things we want to ourselves is not what God wants for us. Many times, we have picked up the wrong things and people in our lives. A lot of hell we bring on ourselves because we get away from our goals and plans. Also, many disassociate themselves with God. *Amos 3:3, "Can two walk together, except they agree."* You must agree with the people you allow in your life. Nevertheless, you must be careful whom you let in your life and befriend. Think of each you have in your life, what are they producing? Are they cranking up your self-confidence? Are they motivating you to excel in life or persuading you to run harder without causing harm? Just notice what they are contributing to your life. Surely, it is something. Wake up; perhaps you have been sleeping too long. These are the most powerful questions that one could ask him or herself. Regardless, if we sometimes do not like the answers, you still must be honest with yourself. After all, why

I can't take one more thing!

cover up reality because it's affecting your life? Do they truly care about you and are they equally showing you the same respect as you give to them? Your friends and love ones should be cranking something greater in you until you begin to achieve things you have always had your heart set on. Simply saying, they should be helping you reach your goals. However, if not, then you are socializing with the wrong people. What are they feeding your mind?

When you are on your way somewhere, you need to get the correct directions. If not, then you may miss your appointment or perhaps simply get lost. So many cannot find their way because they did not take the time to get directions. It is simple, just stop what you are doing and get directions. Plenty of times, I have gotten lost when I was on my way somewhere, but I had to stop and get directions. On the other hand, we allow people to take us down the wrong road of life. Guess what, you still have the opportunity to get back on track. Through daily meditating on the word, you will understand that God has the power to make anything happen right in your life. Job knew though

I can't take one more thing!

his troubles were tormenting him that God could make it all stop. He knew his troubles were only for a season. God wants you to be completely happy with everything in your life. He does not want you upset, lonely, depressed and struggling. God wants to bless your life, and He wants to increase Himself in you. Think about the good things of God and you will get them. *Psalms 23:1 says, The Lord is my Sheppard I shall not want."*

When the assaults tried to take his life, they could not touch his mind. His mind was in position with the will of God. Imagine losing one child, which is enough to make one lose their mind. However, Job lost all at once. An ordinary person cannot relate to Job's situation. Job knew that God was tending over his life. Though his trials were terrible, he was an overcomer. Job did not depend on anyone, not even his wife to stick by his side. He simply depended on God to direct him. For every hard hit of trauma that forced itself into his life, he allowed God to be his Shepherd. Job knew Him as a Tender Shepherd, one that has never failed him and one that has always

I can't take one more thing!

taken care of his needs. You must think with a made up mind on the word. Job had the word working powerfully in his life. That is how he was able to withstand because he walked with the Word. The Word will always stand, even when you fall. The Word will produce when you cannot, and the Word will direct your path. GOD Will Show You The Way.

Job 1:19, "And behold there came a great wind from the wilderness, and smote the four corners of the house, and it fell upon the young men, and they are dead; I only escaped alone to tell thee. Job had received his latest news of devastation." After he had lost everything and almost everyone that he loved. Not only did he lose his children, but their spouses as well. Though he had his wife, she could not stand firm enough by his side to console him. She wanted him to curse his God and die. She just went crazy. Any mother that's lost ten children at once has a right to lose their mind. No one is perfect. I would not even want to understand her pain, it is too painful just thinking about her loss. Perhaps, he could have had grandchildren too. His everyday life was cast away in

I can't take one more thing!

a blink of an eye. Truly, his heart was irritated and broken. There was no medicine made by man to cure his pain. His heart was clawed with intentions to kill. Evidently, his eyes were filled with tears, and sorrowful pain was everywhere. Receiving news worse than bad is a terrible devastation. Not all can handle it! His children were killed in groups at once. Some can bear the pain of losing one, but not all. Job could feel this much grief. The average person could not handle half of what Job endured, and many could not bear a tenth. He had to be strong in the WORD. Though Job had no shoulder to lean on, he immediately fell to worship. It was the worst time of his life. Job only had one true escape from all his life assaults, and it was through his worship. God could only trust Job to bear this kind of affliction. His reward will reflect how significant an actual heavenly return would be. Though many of us suffer from many things, we must feed our mind the WORD. The WORD will inspire you. It will feed your thoughts security and release you from strongholds. *Romans 8:35, "Who shall separate us from the love of Christ?*

I can't take one more thing!

Shall tribulation, or distress, or persecution, or famine, or nakedness, or peril, or sword?" Job was adamant, because his faith was made of steel. Once one goes through the fire, their faith is comparable to steel. Not anything can destroy steel. Steel is molded, welded and shaped through the fire and once it's finished, it is hard to destroy. Although it is dangerously made, it is ready-made to endure. It can go through hail storms, beatings, and everything else. Steel is hard to damage, break, bend or structurally destroy. However, with enough heat it can be RESHAPED! Many of my assaults, caused the ANOINTING to REMAKE ME! I am grateful that I handled all that pressure and was able to be RESHAPED! Perhaps, the heat that is in your life is to RESHAPE you!

Misery loves company, just do not feed it power. When you are aggravated, and things begin to assault your mind, begin to worship. Job did not have time to be angry and worship later, for he worshiped immediately. Often as people, we tend to file complaints first, get angry or think crazy secondly;

I can't take one more thing!

thirdly, most people pray. However, no matter what happens in your life, God wants your worship. In your worst state of mind, He wants you to come directly to Him first. In the most terrible things in your life, God wants you to worship Him first. Only a person that knows Jesus in such a manner can worship Him in terrible living conditions. Job was one that fell to worship the only help he knew. *JOHN 12:25 says, "IF ANY MAN SERVE ME, LET HIM FOLLOW ME; AND WHERE I AM, THERE SHALL ALSO MY SERVANTS BE: IF ANY MAN SERVE ME, HIM WILL MY FATHER HONOUR."*

GOD recognizes an actual good servant that he is entirely pleased with, by rewarding them with heavenly blessing and assurance. God will honor you as He will exalt you with a reward. By showing you a token for your good and letting others see your victory through blessing you. Proving your character and loyalty by being devoted will win you the right to be blessed in many ways. *1 Timothy 5:18, "For the scripture saith, Thou shalt not muzzle the ox that treadeth out the corn. And, the laborer is worthy of his*

I can't take one more thing!

reward." Establishing yourself upon the glorification of CHRIST, will cause you to tread on your enemies and subdue them. When you know Christ personally, no trouble will stop you from going forth in the Word. Desiring to please HIM with all due respect, will be your heart's desire. Because you know that your life is in his hands. Job understood though everything around him was brutally attacked – the Word covered him. We serve an incorruptible God, and His WORDS are everlasting. *Job 28:28, "And unto man he said, Behold, the fear of the Lord, that is wisdom; and to depart from evil is understanding."* Being a true follower of CHRIST, means that you must give no reason to excuse yourself from His WORD. Overcoming power to excel in this life is in His WORD. *Romans 8:35, "Who shall separate us from the love of Christ? Shall tribulation, or distress, or persecution, or famine, or nakedness, or peril, or sword?"* Sometimes I know how things can try to interfere with your devotion, but you cannot begin to allow excuses to submerge your faith walk. As an example, you have prayed for Him to open up the

I can't take one more thing!

windows of Heaven and pour you out a blessing, needing your next miracle to come on time, and He did. When you focus in on the power of GOD, He will take you to a place of assurance that hell could never enter or reach. *Job 1:21, "Naked came I out of my mother's womb, and naked shall I return thither: the Lord gave, and the LORD hath taken away; blessed be the name of the LORD."*

Even during your times of repossessions, losing your possessions, love ones and so on, you must understand that God has the power to bring you in and take you out of this world. He also has the power to rightfully replace things in your life. Job did not expect to take anything out of this world with him, no material possessions, friends or family members. The enemy could not destroy him with that assault because Job knew he came naked into this world and he was prepared to leave naked. He was WORD inclined and knew before hand through the word. Trust Him as Job did. When we all leave this world, we cannot take anything or anyone with us. So, therefore, be grateful for the time you have with love ones and all that God

I can't take one more thing!

allows in your life. Job knew he came into this world naked, and he was prepared not to take anything with him. He knew God had the power over his life regardless of what happened to him. He did not give the enemy any glory. Often during our trials, the first thing we say is that the devil did it. Realistically, the devil must get his authority from God first. Job honored God through it all. Just as marriage vows take place until death do us part, this is the manner in which Job served God even though he had a few imperfections as he served God. Surely, we all do, but God saw Job was perfect and upright. Understand that when you ask God for forgiveness, he has already forgiven you. He wipes your slate clean. Immediately, you appear to Him as blameless. Ask Him for forgiveness and He will. Know how valuable you are to Him, Satan does. No matter what rose up in Job's life, he exalted his Father to be God over it. For better or worse, Job was determined to stay faithful. St. Matthew 16:25 says, *"For whosoever will save his life shall lose it: And whosoever shall lose his life for my sake shall find it."*

I can't take one more thing!

Press your way forth, showing your efforts of desirability. Prove to God that you are a true follower. Give Him the utmost respect. Let nothing or no one interfere with your effort to persevere. *Genesis (22:17&18) "Then shall all nations should eventually call you blessed, because all your dedication will show others your prosperity was gained through your faithfulness?"* Maintain good standards of the Lord your God. After all, He holds the keys to your success. Put your trust in a guaranteed trust, so that God can put His interest in blessings into you. If you show God that you are serious through being faithful, then you will send a message that will put fear in the enemy's heart. The enemy will have to flee away and I mean far away from you. *St. Matthew 16:26, "For what profited a man, if he shall gain the whole world, and lose his soul?" What shall a man give in exchange for his soul?* Ask yourself is again worth it, to lose your only soul? You can replace anything else in your life, but not your soul. For many years, people were blessed with answered prayers. Then shortly afterwards their blessings were received; they too

I can't take one more thing!

turned their backs on GOD. What good is it to get a blessing if you cannot enjoy the benefit or obtain the grace? Being able to be a blessing is the key to operating to live a blessed life. *Genesis 22:17, "In blessings I will bless thee."* Receiving a blessing is good, but being a blessing is far greater. Though Job had gained much in his lifetime, it all still was not worth his soul. Once God blesses you to gain, you must continue to show Him that you appreciate His worth. Desire Him to be God in your life and worship Him. Just as many today are richly blessed, I believe they forget all about who blessed them. Allow Him to bless you, builds you and enlarge you. Do not let what others do cause you to lose your soul or other souls to miss receiving salvation. *Job 29:12 says, "Because I delivered the poor that cried, and the fatherless, and him that had none to help him."*

Job was a constant seeder. He looked down at no one, regardless of his or her condition. He helped many, and his heart was filled with mercy. He knew the depths of reaching down to pull another up through spreading love to all. God wants us to notice the

I can't take one more thing!

conditions of others; to supply their need when it is necessary. A reaper reaps whatever they sow, and Job was a great reaper of great goodness. He missed no seed opportunity, because in planting your seed it shall spring forth and return. Because of Job's devotion to help others, he accumulated greatly. He was not stingy or selfish, but all about helping others. He was one that loved to be a blessing to many that were in need. God wants us all to desire to be a blessing. *Galatians 6:10, "As we have therefore opportunity, let us do good unto all men, especially unto them who are of the household of faith."*

Every time you sow a blessing into someone's life, then you shall receive more than you have sown. GOD will not let you give more than Him. However, He wants us to bless others. For a vine to stay fruitful, the vine must stay connected to the branch. The branch must stay connected to the tree, and the tree must stay rooted. Or else if the vine were removed, then shall it wither up and die. Nevertheless, the vine will not be able to release any more fruit, if it has broken away from the branch. Eventually, the life of

I can't take one more thing!

the vine will die. When you up-root yourself from God, you disconnect yourself from your nurturing lifeline. How can you be enriched, if there is no root? Every plant should be watered to stay refreshed and nurtured or else it will die. *Job 29:13, "The blessings of him that were ready to perish came upon me: and caused the widows heart to sing for joy."* Before the death of his children, Job had prayed for them. God always warns His children, and I believe, He had warned Job. If you look at *Job 29:13,* Job had prepared himself to lose all that he did. I mean everything, after all, he said, "His blessings were ready to die." I know Job prepared himself in worship, word, and prayer before his great lost.

God will send needed people in your path just to check the status of your heart. *Job 29:15, "I was eyes to the blind, and feet was I to the lame."* How you respond towards others in need, by being a blessing, will cause God to bless you greatly. Surely, many are blessed, but they could be blessed far greater by being more of a blessing. Some people are so stingy, selfish and mean until they keep their harvest

I can't take one more thing!

from producing in their life. I survived almost five years without a job, through blessing others. If I needed anything, I just blessed someone else. The word instructs on how to obtain. You are going to reap what you sow. Therefore, if you sow a need, you will reap a need. If you want the doors of heaven to fill your life with blessings, then try being a blessing to others. *(Genesis 22:17)* "Bless people and be grateful that you are able to." Job appreciated his blessings so much until he shared his blessings with others that needed one too. God continued to overflow his increase, because Job had a heart to bless others. Whatever they needed, he was able to provide to them. At no time did Job ask them to repay him for what he provided. He knew God was going to increase him because he was a seeder of good deeds as well as good seeds. You must seed if you expect an increase. *Job 29:14 says, "I put on righteousness, and it clothed me: my judgment was a robe and a diadem."* Can you imagine wearing righteousness for your daily outfit? Job dressed in righteousness every day for everywhere he went. A person that can wear righteousness in the

I can't take one more thing!

manner Job did and would not have a worry or need. Everything will be perfect. Because, trust will cover them everywhere they go for everyday of the week and the rest of their lives. Don't leave home without dressing in righteousness! Job dressed in righteousness. He was royalty to the people everywhere he went. He was covered for the many blessings he bestowed upon the needy. He was blessed to be a blessing and he loved blessing whosoever needed him. He knew Jesus was going to reward him, for being obedient to being a blessing to the needy.

For you to live life to the fullest, continue to feed your mind HIS word. Is your soul worth your house, job, car, spouse, friends, parties, loved ones or even laziness? Why work so hard to gain so little and still lose it all in the end? Everything you put before GOD, you make it God over your life. No amount of things shall be worth your soul, do not give up now. Just continue to press your way and see what your magnificent end is going to be. Many try to prove a point just to be noticed. Now is the time to set it all aside and show to GOD that you want a new mind,

I can't take one more thing!

new ways, a new hope, new territory, and new plans for your new life as well as a new direction. Everything your heart has ever desired can be yours. If only you let GOD prove to you that HE is who HE says HE is. You will never have another worry. Stop holding on to your blessings and release it by being a blessing. Job wore righteousness well. His mercy for others astounded God. *Job 29:15, "I was eyes to the blind, and feet was I to the lame."* It is very simple to live a good life, and it is so much easier to bear the truth of the word. Be a witness and gain trust from GOD. Job helped lead the blind out of poverty. The ones that were blind, literally speaking of anyone that needed direction. He was always willing and prepared to lend a helping hand to pick someone up. Perhaps, Job had experienced rock bottom because his compassion for others was precious and priceless. Job gave them guidance. He shared the WORD, because he desired to help others. He was faithful being a servant to the needy. Just follow the directions of what the Lord tells you and take the time to listen. When you see someone down, pick them up. Do what is in

I can't take one more thing!

your power to help them. I will never forget when I began to sell my books in this particular barbershop. This man said to me, "if you mess up when you get big and I see you, I'm going to throw my hand up, turn my head and look the other way." I immediately said, "If you see me down, help lift me up and pray for me. I'm not perfect." God wants your heart right in Him, righteous is something you wear, it can fit anyone. It does not discriminate. It loves and one size fits all! Love is an action speaking without words. Help those that are less fortunate than you are. Help those that are down and out and bless those that are in need. Job blessed so many people. He was convinced that God would return to him what he has blessed others with. In every seed we sow, God will give us performance. The word of God brings life. Let the word of God clothe you. Once you wear the word, it will speak life to many. Our purpose is to introduce Jesus to the walking dead. In addition, bless as many as you can with love and have compassion. You never know who is going to bless you. Job was one that had compassion without discriminating. *Job 27:6, "My righteousness I*

I can't take one more thing!

hold fast, and will not let it go: my heart shall not reproach me so long as I live." Regardless, Job did not let anything or anyone change the love he had for people. Do not fear the word, but fear the Lord. Every day God gives us the opportunity to sow good seeds in another's life. Often times many sow the wrong seeds. For example, I once heard one say to another, in a derogatory manner, I thought you were a preacher? Instead of that person saying what they thought he was, they should have prayed for their wrongs. Jesus never wasted time by saying what He thought. He acted upon the powers He had. As Jesus healed, He never took the time to think of their wrongs. He automatically begins delivering them. He did not waste time by telling the blind that they were blind, but simply believing that He had the power to restore sight. You and I have the same power. Daily, we all should be encouraging someone that is down, and helping the lame walk. Show them the POWERS You Walk In! It is a dangerous thing to speak against any woman or man of the household of faith. Every time we speak down about someone, we simply let God

I can't take one more thing!

know that He does not have the power to change that individual. If God can call a murderer to lead many out of the land of Egypt, then why can't He call a sinner to repentance? One thing I know, God has a mighty way of making many people eat their own words. When one is trying to do good, that is an opportunity that God has to receive greater glory. So therefore, sow good seeds of all sorts, because after all you have to reap the benefit of whatever you sow. People often wondered how Job was blessed the way he was. His seeds caused him to be blessed. *(Genesis 22:17)* "For every seed he sowed, God multiplied him." If you do not believe this, try it for yourself. For the next 30 days of your life, begin to bless people, just because. After all, how long would you survive off your seeds if you had to? Blessing others will cause blessings to flow and operate in your life. Job lived this scripture, it is another word that brought forth life. *Genesis 22:17, "That in blessing I will bless thee, and in multiplying I will multiply thy seed as the stars of the heaven, and as the sand which is upon the sea-shore; and thy seed shall possess the gate of his*

I can't take one more thing!

enemies." This scripture also caused my life to increase as I needed God to bless me. I did not want to work, because I was working on writing my visions. If I had gone back to work, I would not have had the time to put into writing my ideas. So therefore, I tried this scripture and it worked marvelously in my life. Every time I needed a blessing, I sowed a blessing. Some were in the form of groceries, gas to friends, and money to those that were in need. They did not have to ask me. Just listening with your heart in conversation, was enough to inspire my heart to be moved. I do not expect to ask God for every need, because I expect Him to supply all my needs. Some I have asked for and others He just blessed me with. This is how Job lived such a blessed life, by being a blessing to all that he was able to bless. You must learn the depth of being a blessing. Take off selfishness and put on righteousness. It will clothe your life with every need. I have seen so many relationships die because of selfishness. It is a terrible thing when friends and loved ones know your needs and will not bless you. Listen with your heart. People should not have to ask

I can't take one more thing!

you, your heart should be motivated to do good deeds. One thing I realized is that your income or money will not always be dependable. There may come a time your only way of survival will be your seed survival.

Job 29:3, "When his candle shined upon my head, and when by his light I walked through darkness." Job knew the experience of walking through the valleys of the shadow of death, depending solely on God to be his light and sight. His compassion for others grew greatly from his experience. Perhaps, Job knew what it meant to be without stuff, things, food, and material possession. After he had accumulated so much wealth, he helped others. We all know what it means to suffer, so bless another and watch how you will be blessed. When you go through rough times, you would not want anyone to experience what you have. So therefore, have great compassion. You know God has been there for you in your darkest hours and your worst times. Just spread blessings. The more you bless is, the more God's blessings will bless you! *Job 21:6, "Even when I remember I am afraid, and trembling taketh hold on*

I can't take one more thing!

my flesh." Remember, Job also survived off his seeds and deeds. Your seed has power to even deliver you in a fearful situation. There were many days when I could not see my way during my trying times, and I know my seeds caused me to be delivered. When I was previously on top, I was a blessing to many. Times when I really needed a blessing, God allowed someone to bless me. We all are sowing some kind of seeds, just sow good ones. Whatever you sow is what you shall reap. Sow good seeds and do good deeds!

Job 21:6, "Even when I remember I am afraid, and trembling taketh hold on my flesh." When the strongholds of your life are stronger than you, then you need the actual strength you have never known. You need the strength of a Shield to protect you from the fiery darts of life. You need a mountain Rock, to cover you when the forces of the enemy are roaring against you and the Oil of your Butter to give you sliding ability. A King that can give you precise direction, lead you out of the pattern of destruction; also, a Shepherd to look after you when you are headed in harm's way. He is a Judge that will correct

I can't take one more thing!

you when you are inconceivably wrong; a Refuge that will fight your battle during the times you give up. He has a Fortress of power that you can gain victorious strength of the highest capacity. He is an Avenger to avenge your death in the case of a wounded heart, and He has the power to demolish any weapon that has formed against you. Our Heavenly Father is a Creator that can speak anything into existence. He is someone that has the availability that will surely deliver you out of any situation because you believed without a shadow of doubt against the enemy of confusion. He is a Miraculous Healer when the doctors tell you there is nothing that they can do, because He is the Savior of all the earth. He's a Protector from all hurt, harm, danger, and evil. He is a Provider of sufficiency so that every need in your life will be bountifully met and met on time, and a Redeemer to awaken any dead thing within you so that your soul will be granted the Eternal Life promised with pure happiness and peace. He is my Prince of Peace. He is Mercy forever more and full of Grace. Also, Jesus is the truth, always showing me the way towards His marvelous Light.

I can't take one more thing!

Aggravated Assault On Your Mind

> *"The best is yet to come, run conqueror run!"*
>
> *~Parice Parker*

I can't take one more thing!

Aggravated Assault On Your Mind

CHAPTER 5
Future Effects of Breaking Through

> *"Let Your Faith Possess Your Destiny!"*
> *~ Parice C. Parker*

I can't take one more thing!

CHAPTER 5

Future Effects of Breaking Through

Your mind is generating daily off either negative or positive energy flow. It is transmitting your mind capability into selecting a source of direction and guiding your daily thinking performance towards your life's futuristic results. Also, speaking without showing actions proves nothing! The choices you make today, add consequences for your life tomorrow. Choices do affect your future! *Luke 24:49, "Tarry until ye are endued with power from on high."* Where there is no hope, then tomorrow will already be difficult to face. Truly, where there are no efforts, then

I can't take one more thing!

there is nothing positive to look advance. However, activating your thoughts by showing action speaks louder than words could ever say. It is similar to receiving a visa card with a substantial credit limit, during the time you need it the most. However, when you try to swipe the card nothing happens because you forgot to activate it. Also, some cards require a pin number, and you forgot that too. What good is the card, without it being activated? Activate your power with The Holy Spirit, through the WORD! What good is the Word, if you do not activate it? Just because you put the effort in, it must still be the right effort! Look forward to a positive life, and just delete the negative. Some things and people you probably should have already deleted. Stop holding on to things and individuals that keep you aggravated and upset.

Negative energy is critical towards effectiveness. It disapproves of spiritual growth and advancing in life. Negative energy will cause hindrance, and it will block your prosperity. If you never develop in life, soon you will begin to be aggravated. Negative forces bring about tiredness and laziness that will only

I can't take one more thing!

destroy the mind. I use to have this friend that was very negative. I tried to keep our friendship out of kindness, but their negative spirit begins to destroy me. However, I remember every time this friend came around bad things start to happen. You name it. It happened! I did not realize it at first. However, eventually, I realized this friend had many bad spirits. I invited them into my life. Boy, I was almost destroyed. I went through a hard time after a hard time and eventually I stopped hanging with this particular individual. Often in our relationships, we do not realize that we welcome their spirit world into ours. Consequently, negative energy has the power to destroy you. Being aggravated with life is enough to desire a change. You must run harder towards the mark of your prize. When you reach the supremacy heights that God has designed for you, then you will be endued with His awesome power. Also, your reward will be well worth the affliction. *Proverbs 10:11, "The mouth of a righteous man is a well of life: but violence covereth the mouth of the wicked."* Your choice of people that you allow in your life needs to be

I can't take one more thing!

bringing forth a well of good life. Stay connected to the ones that have his or her mind aiming in the right way. Your future depends on the choices you make today. It does not matter, what walls you have to break through, just move forward! The one thing you need to keep in mind if you do not get through this, then you will never get to your destiny.

Be careful from this day forward whom you entangle yourself with because Your future depends on it. You will either begin to break through or stay in bondage, due towards the company you keep. Remember nothing from nothing, leaves nothing. The more you allow God to dispense His power through you, the more powerful you will become. Zero The Almighty out and your prosperity will be zeroed out as well. Now, if God is working mightily through you and He too should be working the same through your associates. If not, you will soon have a problem. *Amos 3:3, "Can two walk together, except they are agreed?"* When two are in agreement, those things will come even if it is negative. How can you ever be generated with effective energy source? Accept the

I can't take one more thing!

facts. Socializing with negative people that have no vision, will simply hold you down. Honestly, they will also hinder your progress. Tally up your associates, because who and whatever they are you will soon become! Also, whatever is on their mind is going to affect yours. If they have nothing to hope for, then how are you going to be encouraged or how are you going to encourage them? Can the blind lead the blind? One needs a pair of eyes just to help lead the other where they need to be. Realistically speaking, if you take a moment and look at your associates. Itemize them and then calculate yourself. What are they adding in or subtracting out of your life? What is their purpose of association with you? Is it something positive or negative? Have you figured this equation? A drunk should not hang with a top notch CEO or a prostitute with the president. It just does not add up; neither is it appropriate. It is vital whom you associate with because positive energy promotes and negative energy demotes. When your associates are around you, what and who are you representing? When they leave your presence, what reflection have they left on you?

I can't take one more thing!

How well do you prepare yourself for them? Are they helping you to be a better you? Why delay your progress? Also, why should you allow anyone that power in your life, to the time lag your advancement? Evidently, Job went through enough, but what if he would have permitted his friends to keep him in bondage? Perhaps, he would have never received double for his trouble and probably he would have missed his appointment with obtaining his new life. Think about his wife, how she too went against him. He did not let her stop him either. *Proverbs 27:17, "Iron sharpeneth iron; so a man sharpeneth the countenance of his friend."* The truth is that your associates are going to extend their sharpness into your life, as well as you to theirs. You want people in your life that are always preparing themselves to be blessed. Once one is truly blessed, they can soon bless others. Your associates should be causing you to desire to be more than a conqueror. They should be encouraging you to give up the wrong, for the right. Also, you should be running the race of becoming a winner with an accurate determination. Allow your

I can't take one more thing!

association to help sharpen you, well as you sharpen them. If none is happening, then flee now! Your life progress depends on it! One example is when I use to sing at our church; the members would put me down. They often tore at my trying ability. If you surround yourselves with people that cannot see beyond your effort, then shake the dust off and move forward. If you keep hanging with individuals with no vision, they will blind you too. Stop letting people hold you back. What if I had let people cause me to stop, my spiritual development would have stopped too. It is valuable not to be around the wrong people; they will keep your prosperity in a lock down the position. Be around those that will appreciate your effort and the ones that will build your confidence. All you need is for someone to see your good, look beyond your faults and feel your energy. A true friend, believer or love one will help you sharpen the tools that God has given you. If you hold back on God, it will only cause you to be held back. Are you tired of aggravated assaults? Associate yourself around the righteous and you will begin to see real movement and progress in your life.

I can't take one more thing!

Proverbs 10:11, "The mouth of a righteous man is a well of life: but violence covereth the mouth of the wicked." Prepare yourself to embrace the power of GOD. It is a good way to offset negative people. Conclude to the point you now want security. Stake out your surrounding area as you focus that will assure you of no malfunction. Consistently, check all necessary vital points. Keep your mind focused on the productive powers of JESUS. HE has all power in HIS hands. Wherever HIS power is, then your mind must also be. Stay encouraged. The power of GOD is real, and so is HIS presence. HE increases the weak to be strengthened with wisdom. It heals at all times, motivates your most vulnerable areas, and it produces power from on high.

Having a determined mind will make you seek the power of God. It will cause you to prepare to work your faith as never before. Surely, faith without works is dead. Your hope for tomorrow depends on your faith today. That is why it is imperative to stay tuned in with RIGHTEOUSNESS. The Holy Spirit feeds your mind power to keep you insured with the right

I can't take one more thing!

thinking capability. *Job 29:5 says When the Almighty was yet with me when the secret of God was upon my tabernacle.* As Job was a child, He was adequately trained through The Spirit of God. Job was a walking tabernacle for The WORD. He did not need a church to make him worship or praise. Everywhere Job went, he carried his tabernacle. In it were his faith, belief, and power. God reveals His secrets only to His own. Job spent quality time in secret with God, as The Holy Spirit fed Him. Once you go to God in secret, He will whisper many Anointing things in your ear. It is an excellent gift, to receive revelation. Not everyone can hear from The Holy Spirit. Satan cannot either that is why He is so angry with you. He does not want you to hear God; you will find out his secrets. Also, it holds the power to rebuke him, stop him and to cancel him out of your life. That is why he wants you separated from The Word. Because once you get it, you will be able to run and be more than a conqueror. Job was one that God revealed Himself. Think of your relationship with your husband or wife. No one knows your secrets as they do. Some things you will not feel comfortable

I can't take one more thing!

sharing with a stranger, especially personal things. This kind of relationship requires intimate privacy. When you get intimate with The Holy Spirit, there will be a seal on your life. Do Not Disturb! No one will have the power to open your door. Regardless, what you are going through you will be able to rest quietly and be peaceful. The more you go in your secret place is, the greater your communication grows with God. A husband and a wife can reveal themselves to one another that others cannot. That is the manner God wants you to explain yourself to Him in secret, and He will reveal Himself to you. He only shares His secrets with the ones He finds trustworthy. That is why they receive His favor and power to subdue. Prove yourself to Him, as Job did. Let Jesus know that you are not His enemy. *Job 6:8, "Oh that I might have my request; and that God would grant me the thing that I longed for!"* Make sure your eyes remain on everything that is positive. Never take it off your request. Allow your mind to stay in position to see your petition, feel your application until you can touch your request become evident. It is time to move on

I can't take one more thing!

your application. To be insured by active power, you must connect to positive things including positive people. Yes, a plus here and a plus there adds up!

During Job conversation with Eliphaz, one of his friends, Job stood through his grief with hope in God. Though Eliphaz tried to discredit him, Job did not slack down. If it appears to be crucial in your life and impossible for someone else, remember you must continue to believe that it will happen. People will question your faith, but it does not mean that you need to. *Job 6:8, "Oh that I might have my request; and that God would grant me the thing that I longed for!"* Your power line is your primary driven source of positive energy. It will link you to The Holy Spirit. Anything that is not of JESUS will corrupt your future. It will cause distractions when you try to call upon Jesus. Those distractions will sometimes tie up your connection with The Holy Spirit. It is the time that you take extreme precautions, of who you are socializing with on a daily basis. Having the inverse association in your life, will cause conflict between you and God. They are going to help you stay in tune

I can't take one more thing!

with The Holy Spirit, or they are going to cause confusion in your life. The bad association will cause your faith to decrease. The Spirit knows the Spirit by the Spirit. The key to your success is overcoming life, full of aggravations. If your daily associates are lusting after the things of Heaven, then you are in the right company. On the other hand, that company may cause you to leave God alone. Friendship goes deeper than you think! Your friends also help guide your future. They can either cause you to be exalted or buried. I do not want a friend that is going to dig a hellhole for me. Friends can cause you to live right or bad, and there is no in between. Associates will change your life and cause you to change. It is so deep; associations pertain the keys to your destiny! Some people will keep aggravation stirred up in your life, and it is not worth it. Many get off on your aggravations. Oh, this greatly inspired my heart when Job said, "mark me and be astonished." Those kinds of people are powerless, and they have no faith. Let them be miserable alone. Many have talked about me. Who cares? Because while they were talking and marking me with their powerless

I can't take one more thing!

words. God was putting His mark on my life. Mark me and be astonished. I love it because it gets God brewing more in me. *Psalms 105:15 says, Touch not my anointed and do my prophet no harm.*

Job 29:20, "My glory was fresh in me, and my bow was renewed in my hand." Once you begin to associate with The Almighty, He will put the things you will need in the palms of your hands. Just as He gave Job power to overcome, He will do the same for you. Every time you bow in reverence to The Almighty, you will gain power. Reverence our CREATOR. Job was always being renewed, as the troubles of his life blew with great forces. It only pushed him to gain greater sustaining ability. If you need a miracle, go and bow down to The Almighty and rise with your miracle. Regardless of your need, God is the greatest association you need. He has a weapon of power designed for every single assault that could ever possibly aggravate you. He is your WEAPON, and His WORD will be your DEFENSE. Pursue your relationship with Him. Get to know Him deeply. Let Him tell you His secrets, because there is

I can't take one more thing!

conquering power that will demolish every dirty thing in your life. Job understood God secrets. They were sweet to his ear. It was his smooth operating power to slide through every troubled time with victory. Job knew because WISDOM granted him power from The Most High. He let the secrets of God dwell deep in him, which made Job generous in spirit and wealthy in substance! That is why so many could not understand, how Job continued to stand through all his devastation. God is rich in mercy, and He is everlasting joy. Job knew how wealthy his Heavenly Father was. *Ephesians 3:20 says, Now unto him that can do exceeding abundantly above all that we ask or think, according to the power that worketh in us.* Job had power, because he had the WORD, working in and through him.

Hindering Blocks of Effectual Prayer:

- *Lack of Knowledge (Proverbs 8:33-35), Ecclesiastes 2:26)*
- *Planning & Preparation Write The Vision (Habakkuk 2: 2-4)*

I can't take one more thing!

- *The Wrong Association (Amos 3:3)*
- *Laziness (Proverbs 10:4)*
- *No Vision (Proverbs 29:18 & John 3:16)*
- *Fear of Faith (Hebrew 11:6), Proverbs 13:12*
- *Being Made Over (Hebrew 1:4)*
- *Fear of The LORD (Proverbs 14:27 & Job 28:28)*

Get serious and be determined. Set your new dialogue and allowing The Holy Spirit to lead your life. God wants to give you abundance, through your spiritual growth. Begin your day with gladness. Rejuvenate your mind to become more than a conqueror. I believe Job knew from the moment his life was assaulted with claws of intentions to kill. He was secure in his faith through The WORD. *Proverbs 13:11, "Hope deferred maketh the heart sick, but when desire cometh, it is a tree of life."* He did not pray now and believed later. His desire to overcome kept his faith thinking a better day is coming. An excellent example of deferred hope is deferred

I can't take one more thing!

payment. Simply means you will pay later, with more interest added to that debt on the latter end. The way Job had hope was an immediate debt paid in full. No matter what you are going through, once your heart begins to desire something, it will spark your hope. Job wanted to come out greater than he went in. He was conscious of his faith. He was a believer. *Job 6:8, "Oh that I might have my request; and that God would grant me the thing that I longed for!"* Through the word, you shall be endued. Continue feeding your mind wisdom. Inter- lock your mind with the word. It will spiritually motivate you towards provision, which will cause you to make significant progress. Get to know God through the Holy Spirit. For it has the Greatest Power of all. The Holy Spirit will increase your mind to stay confidence in The WORD. Thinking with a mind prepared for receiving all that GOD has stored up and waiting for you. *(I Corinthians 2:9)* Get aggravated enough to be tired of being violated, through the enemy's traps. Let your mind exalt in The Word, as it will increase to think more powerfully. When your mind upset, your vision will feel the

I can't take one more thing!

pressure, and you will hardly have movement. Let nothing stop your zeal. Want to be able to make a difference in lives, from this day forward. Your prayer power is your direct source of connection to GOD'S power surge. Prayer is not only for making your request known; it is your only accessible interlink to operate in the strength of The Holy Spirit. To pray, you must first recognize the power that prayer holds. He created the world and you through the might of His Power. That is the kind of God you will be praying.

Job 16:17, "Not for any injustice in my hands: also my prayer is pure." God wants you to have a pure prayer life. As you pray, He wants solitude. Focus on Him! Your power is in His might. Prayer will increase your weakest areas in life, and it will build you. Prayer will bring forth stability, as it will stabilize your faith in JESUS. Job was a stabilized servant. He knew God in secret, through prayer. When you think spiritually, then God will produce heavenly things in your life. Prayer will take you out of self and place you with the powers of God. It is your access to His powers. Things will not aggravate you because you will be allowing

I can't take one more thing!

God to take care of your troubles. Prayer will comfort your soul in troubled times, and it will give you strength. It will allow you to bear things out of the ordinary. Job was one that prayed to God with a pure heart. When you pray, let it be a pure heart prayer. Job allowed The Holy Spirit to dwell in his tabernacle! *Psalms 15:1, "LORD, who shall abide in thy tabernacle?* Who shall dwell in thy holy hill?" During prayer, you will be able to live in the presence of The LORD. His Holy presence is power from on high. That is why Job was able to tolerate so much. Satan might have many tricks and treats, but he does not have Holy Wisdom! Get your Holy WISDOM and be empowered. Afterward, look at your life. I guarantee a Divine Increase and favor from The highest will be president in your life!

Revelation 21:6, "And he said unto me, It's done." I am Alpha and Omega, the beginning and the end. I will give unto him that is a thirst of the fountain of the water of life freely. He is your Alpha and Omega. It's done! Once you realize who He is, then you can begin your pure prayer towards heaven. Notice that

I can't take one more thing!

whenever God allow heaven to open, there must be generous over flow of RIGHTEOUSNESS. It will descend on your behalf. Prayer teaches one responsibility, enhances your mind capability, and develops your sense of magnitude. Prayer also creates an unconditional love, within your heart to be more compassionate towards others. It gives you power over all of your strong holds. It is your guidance tool of assurance, towards perfection. Prayer is the greatest weapon of defense to fight the wiles of your enemies.

When times are troubled in your life that is when you need to draw closer to God and not further away. *Job 1:22, "In all this Job sinned not, nor charged God foolishly."* I have seen too many people mess up their lives because trouble popped up in their life. Many have taken a ride on the worst life roller coasters, with no intention of stopping. From drugs to violence, alcohol to abuse, profanity to life courses and so much more. Their life turned from good to worst, all because of aggravated assault on the mind. Also, they were associating with the wrong people! Many are lost and cannot find their way back. Only, because, they quit

I can't take one more thing!

praying! Never quit praying! *(1 Thessalonian 5:17), "Pray without ceasing." Many have stopped The Holy Spirit from being invited into their lives.* Only the Anointing destroys the yokes. Satan has fooled so many people and caused them not to believe in the power of prayer. It works! Make sure you never stop praying! Your strength to get through this thing is to be plugged up with The Holy Spirit. The worst thing we can do, when trouble arises in our life is left God's side. He is the only one that has the power to bring forth peace and denounce trouble. You cannot fight Satan with Satan. You must fight Satan with the POWER of The Holy Spirit. Satan may fight you, but he cannot defeat Jesus. You are already defeated against Satan if you do not have heavenly powers! Staying connected with Jesus will continuously cause you to be SAVED, repeatedly! Satan cannot compare to Jesus Powers. Job knew that sin would destroy his communication with The Holy Spirit. Sin is destruction, and it destroys one's hope. A sincere prayer irritates the enemy because it causes God to move. There are not many that can cause the hand of

I can't take one more thing!

The Highest, to move. The heart that is true will cause valleys to be exalted and mountains to be made low! Moreover, it assassinates the followers of the enemy. Giving them no defeat over you! Prayer is your vital point through the feeding tube of the WORD. It endangers the enemy and destroys your flesh. A pure prayer life will remove all ungodly intolerance's out of your pathway. Your heart will flame holy fire. Your waywardness will not hinder you. Because you will be effectual, and prayer will correctly line you up with the will of God. Holding ought or wickedness within your heart is a devastation mark towards your prayer life with GOD.

Just because someone has upset you, or you disagree with their personalities, does not mean that you should hate them. Ask GOD for forgiveness from your heart and forgive them of their wrong doings. As GOD forgives us more times in our life, then you and I could ever count in seven lifetimes. Just have a forgiven heart towards others. GOD is not a weak GOD. Though Satan comes to tempt us, does not mean we should engage. Think for a moment. JESUS even

I can't take one more thing!

needed to pray when Satan tempted Him. So, we should be praying even harder. Remember, before Satan tempted JESUS on the mountaintop. He too had been in deep prayer. He communed with heaven. He too allowed heaven to strengthen his ability to withstand all the enemies' temptations. So, who are you not to need God? We all need Him to overcome temptation. Your mind needs daily spiritual supplication. A pure prayer life will cause you to gain double for your trouble.

Proverbs 3:6, "In all thy ways acknowledge him, and he shall direct thy paths." Allow the Powers of God to be your life protector. Give Him access 24 hours a day and seven days a week, to cover you. Keep your access open with Him through daily worship and prayer. As you pray to ask Him to lead you, and allow Him to lead your heart to worship. However, as you pray The Spirit of God will usher His Divine presence into your life. It will take complete control. God can keep, protect, cover and overshadow your family from all, hurt, harm, danger, and evil principalities. Imagine if you were an assailant

I can't take one more thing!

creeping in the midnight hour, your only protective is seeking an easily possible victim. If you miss a morning prayer, then you did not give God complete authorization over your day. If you miss your noonday prayer, then you missed an opportunity of refueling with power from The Holy Spirit. If you missed your evening prayer, then you have missed another chance of gaining more available power from on high. So think for a minute, if The Highest is your God, then treat Him as your (sole & soul) provider. Soon as Abraham was willing to give up his son Isaac as a sacrificial burnt offering. The angel spoke to Abraham: The angel said: "Lay not thine hand upon the lad, neither do anything unto him; for now, I know that thou fears God, seeing thou has not withheld thy son, thine only son from me." Immediately God had provided Abraham with a ram in the bush. Abraham sacrificed his only son for faith; he would deliver. He knew going in with his only son that they would come out together. He listened to The Spirit of God, and he was not selfish. Abraham was willing! Abraham knew that God was going to supply his ram in the bush,

I can't take one more thing!

because of his faith. Just as God supplied Abraham, He will supply you. You must note that He is your contributor, supplier, Giver, donor, and provider of everything. Through your prayer life, He will give you all your needs, even those you forget to ask. That is why prayer is vital. It contributes spiritual development. Prayer will inhabit your faith walk in the Power of God.

For you to achieve in life, then you need available power from on high. Without access, then how shall you receive? You cannot hop from every doctrine and teacher. For the word of God has warned us that in the last day's there will be many preaching and teaching in my name, but they will not be of me. They will bring forth unstableness to your life, for their personal gain. Think realistically for a moment, how many pastors today are concerned about their sheep? The majority of them do not know their sheep's first or last name. Also, if you left the ministry, they probably did not notice you were gone because they hardly see when you are there. You wonder why the enemy has assaulted you. Find a haven where you can be

I can't take one more thing!

spiritually fed through the word of God. You need a WORD teacher, one that hears from The Holy Spirit. I am not speaking of those that will sugar coat your ears with prosperity gain. I am talking about the one that will cause you to move away from sin. No one is perfect; that is why we all must continue to work towards perfection. God wants you to prosper, but He wants you to prosper righteously. He wants you to receive His word, including the words that will cause sin to be removed from your life. Right is right and wrong is wrong. Just as a child eats a lot of candy, eventually their teeth will decay. Well, that is the same effect many ministries have today. Sweet tooth with sugar coated messages and the saints are rotting more and more away! However, I knew this one Pastor as he quoted, "Cotton Candy Preachers." God is a God of truth, and I know the truth sometimes hurt, but it will set you free. God does not want us to gain the whole world and lose our only soul. Ministry should never be focused on money or material things. If God purposed it, surely it will prosper. Though it may not grow when you want it to, it will. You need to know that God is

I can't take one more thing!

real, and He wants us to be made complete in Him. If God speaks to you, then how are you speaking to others?

Job 21:6, "Even when I remember I am afraid, and trembling taketh hold on my flesh." When the strongholds of your life are stronger than you, then you need the actual strength you have never known. You need the strength of a Shield to protect you from the fiery darts of life. You need a mountain Rock, to cover you when the forces of the enemy are roaring against you and the Oil of your Butter to give you sliding ability. A King that can give you precise direction, lead you out of the pattern of destruction; also, a Shepherd to look after you when you are headed in harm's way. He is a Judge that will correct you when you are inconceivably wrong; a Refuge that will fight your battle during the times you give up. He has a Fortress of power that you can gain victorious strength of the highest capacity. He is an Avenger to avenge your death in the case of a wounded heart, and He has the power to demolish any weapon that has formed against you. Our Heavenly Father is a Creator

I can't take one more thing!

that can speak anything into existence. He is someone that has the availability that will surely deliver you out of any situation because you believed without a shadow of doubt against the enemy of confusion. He is a Miraculous Healer when the doctors tell you there is nothing that they can do because He is the Savior of all the earth. He's a Protector from all hurt, harm, danger, and evil. He is a Provider of sufficiency so that every need in your life will be bountifully met and met on time, and a Redeemer to awaken any dead thing within you so that your soul will be granted the Eternal Life promised with pure happiness and peace. He is my Prince of Peace. He is Mercy forever more and full of Grace. Also, Jesus is the truth, always showing me the way towards His marvelous Light.

I can't take one more thing!

Aggravated Assault On Your Mind

"While they are laughing at the marks of the enemy in your life. Truly, God is marking you with His Divine Favor!"

~Parice C. Parker

I can't take one more thing!

Aggravated Assault On Your Mind

CHAPTER 6
Mark Me & Be Astonished

"The Biggest Loser, is Always The Biggest Winner!"
~ *Parice C. Parker*

I can't take one more thing!
CHAPTER 6

Mark Me & Be Astonished

Talk here, smirk and grin there as many laughed at Job living in despair. Ha, ha, ha I knew you were the cause of all this trouble! Many probably said, "I knew he wasn't right." Job heard it all. I can relate to Job as he was afflicted in every area of his life. Though God saw him as upright, people may not have received Job in that manner. God looks at us differently than man. Everyone was probably mocking him. Surely, he was the laughing stock of the century. All his friends begin to put him down, discredit his worth and brutally talk about him. Everywhere he turned, his manhood assaulted, and his self-esteem was under attack. *Job 21:5, "Mark me, and be astonished, and lay your hand upon your mouth."* If it

I can't take one more thing!

were not so, Job would not have quoted this scripture. Job was trying to warn them, watch what you say about me. His example covers your mouth, "you're better off saying nothing." Another one of Satan attempts is to make you appear unworthy. Though man looks on the outward appearance, God is looking at the heart. People must be careful how they treat one that God loves.

Job knew he was already delivered, even as he went through. That is why he told them to mock him. Job knew that God was bringing him out. He was aware that his trials were not going to last always. Although, many were pointing their fingers at me as they laughed about my trials. I saw that some were glad. My Heavenly Father was just refining me, to come out as Gold. Though the people could not understand, Job did. Because, he had already received what God had promised him. Though he was not out yet, he believed in his spirit that he was delivered. The people could not see it yet, but it was done! He stood on The Word! *Job 21:5, "Mark me, and be astonished, and lay your hand upon your mouth."* Many need to watch what

I can't take one more thing!

they say as they speak against a child of The Almighty. Job knew who he was. He also knew whom he served and who was going to bring him out. He may not have known the time or hour, but he was expecting to be delivered at any day. It was all just a matter of time. He warned them to stop talking to him, and they would not. Many bring great trouble to their own lives, by mocking someone else's. *2 Timothy 3:12 says, "Yea, and all that will live godly in Christ Jesus shall suffer persecution."* Whatever words you sow, you too shall reap. *Genesis 12:2 & 3* Blessings follow blessing and curses follow curses. Everyone loves to give their reasons for why you are going through, when things in your life appear bitter. Job was one that was terribly talked about and criticized, when things went haywire in his life. *Job 21:3 "Suffer me that I may speak; and after that I have spoken, mock on."* Be careful what you say about people that are suffering. You never know why they are suffering, and how deep their sufferings are. Most of all, who they are suffering to become! Jesus suffered greatly and He rose up being The Almighty! *(Hebrew 11:25)* Many days I felt

I can't take one more thing!

like Job, I experienced much of what he endured. It was not easy being under extreme attack by everyone and everything at once. Though my experiences were not as traumatizing as Job's, it was more than enough for me to handle. *Romans 8:17 says, "And if children, then heirs, heirs of God, and joint-heirs with Christ; if so be that we suffer with him, that we may be also glorified together."* Nevertheless, I overcame. When I just needed someone to say I love you, I felt attacked. When I needed to hear a word of encouragement, they talked about me. Everywhere I went, I heard them speaking and laughing at me. All alone in my mind, I said, "If Only They Knew!" You never know whose suffering for Righteousness, and what they are becoming. *Romans 8:18, "For I reckon that the sufferings of this present time are not worthy to be compared with the glory which shall be revealed in us."* People do not understand, the righteous are required to suffer! The righteous simply go through hell, just to be made right! We must, in order to be able to endure and develop a deeper trust in the name of Jesus. *Proverbs 18:10, "The name of the LORD is*

I can't take one more thing!

a strong tower: the righteous runneth into it, and is safe." In order to be developed in righteousness, you will endure great affliction. I mean the kind of ailment that can cause you to question is God real? *(11 Timothy 3:12)* Yes, your life will be under great attack. Satan's purpose is to destroy you. When one is under attack, they must run to safety. Job ran to The Almighty and He kept Job safe. Let the Word fight your assailants. Trust that this assault will soon be over and you will overcome being a wealthy winner!

Surely, Satan is going to throw everything he can at you. Job, understood. *11 Timothy 3:13, "But evil men and seducers shall wax worse and worse, deceiving, and being deceived."* One of Satan's greatest attempts is to seduce the believer through mocking words. He loves it when a believer is tempted by simple things to cause their faith to weaken. He likes to stir up people to talk to you, because the best way to get the word out is through word of mouth. Satan wants the WORD of The Most High out of you, as well as he wants the word about you out! He loves it when children of The Righteous begin to look as though no God is in them.

I can't take one more thing!

That is when the mocking begins, as people advertise your troubles! *Job 21:3 Suffer me that I may speak; and after that I have spoken, mock on.* If men only knew, that the righteous must suffer before they rise up. Biblically speaking, before all rose up, including Jesus, many truly suffered. Before one can genuinely represent The Righteous, one must experience being a partaker of long suffering. *1 Peter 4:13 says, but rejoice, inasmuch as ye are partakers of Christ's sufferings; that, when his glory shall be revealed, ye may be glad also with exceeding joy.* Job was expecting a great reward after his long suffering was over. We are born first of our mother's womb. Secondly, we must be born through The Spiritual Womb of Righteousness. Everyone cannot handle this birth, many are aborted. Many will simply be stillborn, while others will be righteously birthed. However, before Righteousness births you – you must be spiritually born! The righteous is not made for all to survive in coming through. It is the toughest birth of your life and a slim canal to slide through. Before anyone can make it through this spiritual womb, the

I can't take one more thing!

person must be just right for Jesus to birth him or her through. *Job 31:15, "Did not he that made me in the womb make him?* And did not one fashion us in the womb?" You cannot be too big, for then you must be humbled. You cannot be too grown, for you must be born as a babe. In addition, when you are born, you will be covered with The Blood of the Lamb. Before new birth can appear, there must be a new development that will cause you to spiritually mature. Suffering for the righteous is self-explanatory. A fine example, you find out who is truly by your side when you are being afflicted, from being sick to losing stuff in life. Perhaps, falling down will cause you to want to get back up. When you are down, look up and see who is standing by your side. People will drop you like a bad habit, just to get rid of you. They will disappear when you need them the most. Believe me, I know and I believe that is why we must suffer so. Jesus wants to know who is by His side. You know there are many fake people in this world. What if tomorrow, you were blessed with a great wealth? Would you want to bless the people that walked out of your life, when you

I can't take one more thing!

needed them the most? Would you bless those that stuck by your side, through thick and thin? Surely, you would bless those accordingly as they deserve. That is the same thing we must understand, a test of who we are and the purpose of our endeavor. Many could not suffer by the side of Jesus and still consider Him their God. Only a select few! However, Job did. He had a unique love for The Almighty. Because once righteousness becomes a part of your development, old things must pass away. The new man of righteousness begins to take place. This new man will not be able to wear the things he used to, it simply will not fit! It will no longer be a comfort, but a pestilence. A transformation will begin to take place that no one would be able to see. That is why Satan is using the hell on the outside of your life, because he cannot see what God is doing inside. However, God purposely wanted their eyes on your outer appearance, because he was dissecting and rearranging your inner man. He has begun a Supernatural Spiritual Transplant from heaven inside you. Through your afflictions, He is giving you a more loving heart, a determined mind

I can't take one more thing!

and a better attitude. Your whole inside is being spiritually remodeled, while others are mocking you. He is working all hell out of your life. Though you know what is going on inside, they do not. Well, Job understood. He simply knew that newness was taken place in His life. Remember, God was already well pleased with Job beforehand.

Sometimes to others, it will seem like God is not answering you, because the way your life has appeared.

Job 15:4, (word from Eliphaz to Job) "Yea, thou castest off fear, and restrainest prayer before God." Do not worry about what others say, think or wonder about you. Just keep your heart pure with God at all times. More often, many do not realize a mighty warrior must fight a mighty battle, to be known as a mighty conqueror. Things may come to torment your life, but it is all to make you stronger and wiser - as Jesus implants Himself in you. 1 *John 4:4, "Ye are of God, little children, and have overcome them: because greater is he that is in you, than he that is in the*

I can't take one more thing!

world." Many will go against you just as Job's closest friends and wife did, but he continued to pray. This battle is not easy and only the strong will survive. It is a terrible thing, when your life is assaulted from every angle and no one is by your side, not even your spouse. I know how Job grew extremely lonely, well as his pain unbearable. Once I went through the roughest storm of my life. Actually, before one storm was over another begin. Many nights I tossed and turned. No one could truly imagine all I went through at once. My storm began in 2000 and each year the winds blew more forceful. Eventually, all I had was the WORD and my Savior. My storm lasted for many years. The more I opened my eyes, the less loved ones I saw. Friends, who? I can't hear you, who? I found out the hard way, who cared about me. The hardest thing to bear is getting to know Jesus, spiritually! No strength is greater, than our Heavenly Father's. Job too understood that. *Job 21:3 "Suffer me that I may speak; and after that I have spoken, mock on."* Through Job's suffering he too could be acquainted with The Holy Spirit. However, long-suffering was his testimony and

I can't take one more thing!

his testimony was his proof. After all, his going through and coming out was enough to speak for itself. He knew his life was going to be a powerful reflection. Billions and zillions have reflected in his testimony during their time of need. He never was concerned about his troubles, because he gave that burden to God. Honestly, his life has helped me repeatedly. In addition, I know today that it is helping you too. Every time I read the book of Job, I am greatly inspired. God is your strength, if you let Him be your source. He will not leave you alone and soon, He will repay you for all your troubles. I too suffered greatly as others mocked me with their many babbling words. Truly, I appeared to be unworthy and at first, I could not understand. I cried out, why me and I heard a voice say, "Why Not you?!" I felt many aggravations as I strived to do good. Just keep in mind, God has not forgotten you. Hold on to God in prayer and He will eventually release your rewards. Every prayer will soon be answered, just hold on. God is just making you stronger. As many mocked Job, they will mock you too. Still, keep in mind as the

I can't take one more thing!

mock goes on that you are a trophy winner. If you have not receive it by now, then God is still making you greater. Many are soon going to be astonished. *Psalms 140:13, "Surely the righteous shall give thanks unto thy name: the upright shall dwell in thy presence."* I could not have kept my eyes on my troubles and survival too. I just kept my mind focused on surviving. I did not have time to worry about whom and what I had lost. I was too busy in the WORD. I refused to attempt to fight a battle that is not mine. So therefore, my life battles I give to the LORD. Once you get tired of crying, you will wipe those tears away and get busy surviving. Let God fight your battles. Why deal with something that can kill you. It is not worth running your blood pressure up, having a stroke or a heart attack. Just let the WORD fight your battles.

One thing I realized is to appreciate every assault that has tried me, because it enhanced my faith. I endured and so can you. I thoroughly praised God for every effort that the enemy put against me. Yet, through my most trying times, God was just fortifying my faith. Job endured and so can you. *Job 23:10, "But He*

I can't take one more thing!

knoweth the way I take: when he hath tried me, I shall come forth as gold." I cried many tears when I needed Him the most. God was always there. He always answers me and not a moment too late. Do not look at yourself and think that you can. Only the Almighty has the power to do so. Seek God, in everything in your life. His grace and mercy will keep you. I thank my Heavenly Father for all I had to bear and for every heavy load I had to carry; God has empowered me. Jesus is my strength. Jesus is everything. If it were not for the Lord on my side, then where would I be? I do not even want to know. *Job 21:6, "Even when I remember I am afraid, and trembling taketh hold on my flesh." Jesus covered me.* He protected me through The Storms of Life. It was like the storm of the century. When I could not stand, JESUS stood up in me, and only because of Him I stood! *Job 23:11 says, "My foot hath held his steps, his way have I kept, and not declined."* As Job was tried, he was simply being a righteous example for our Heavenly Father to produce faith for others. As we all look back over Job's life, we can all testify. It was only the LORD. Job's suffering

I can't take one more thing!

was to teach us all to endure patiently. Never rush the work of The Almighty! Let His will be done in your life as it was done in Job's. After all, his latter was far greater than his beginning. Wait I say, and wait with patience on The LORD!

Job 21:3 "Suffer me that I may speak, and after that I have spoken, mock on." When the strongholds of your life are stronger than you, then you need the immediate strength you have never known. You need the strength of a Shield to protect you from the fiery darts of life. You need a mountain Rock, to cover you when the forces of the enemy are roaring against you and the Oil of your Butter to give you sliding ability. A King that can give you perfect direction, lead you out of the pattern of destruction; also, a Shepherd to look after you when you are headed in harm's way. He is a Judge that will correct you when you are inconceivably wrong; a Refuge that will fight your battle during the times you give up. He has a Fortress of power that you can gain victorious strength, of the highest capacity. An Avenger to avenge your death in the case of a wounded heart and He has the power to

I can't take one more thing!

demolish any weapon that has formed against you. Our Heavenly Father is a Creator that can speak anything into existence. Someone that has the availability will surely deliver you out of any situation. Belief without a shadow of doubt will cause it to happen. Miraculous Healer - when the doctors tell you there is nothing that they can do, because He is the Savior of all the earth. A Protector from all hurt, harm, danger, and evil. He is a Provider of sufficiency so that every need in your life will be bountifully met and met on time. A Redeemer to awaken any dead thing within you, so that your soul will be granted the Eternal Life promised with pure happiness and peace. He is my Prince of Peace. He is Mercy forever more and full of Grace. Also, Jesus is the truth, always showing me the way towards His marvelous Light.

I can't take one more thing!
Aggravated Assault On Your Mind

"No Pain, Absolutely No Gain!"

~Parice C. Parker

<u>I can't take one more thing!</u>

Aggravated Assault On Your Mind

CHAPTER 7
Dwell In Safety

> *"Be Untouchable!"*
> *~ Parice C. Parker*

I can't take one more thing!

CHAPTER 7

Dwell In Safety

As I truly look back over my life, all I can say is, "Thank You, Jesus!" No one could tell it as I can. If it was not for the LORD on my side, I do not want to know where I would be. Surely, you can attest to this as well. *Job 23:10, "But He knoweth the way I take: when he hath tried me, I shall come forth as gold."* Many cannot understand while they are going through, that it is all to make a better you come forth. No, I could not figure out what was going on with my life. However, I still held on to my faith. In many cases, I did not have anything to hold onto, but my faith. Surely, Job was one that truly understood. While everyone else was looking and laughing at Job, his troubles were refining him. *Philippians 1:21, "For to me to live is Christ, and to die is gain."* Often, things

I can't take one more thing!

that appear in our lives to hurt us are the very things that are to bless us. For years, I was hurt over the way many things appeared in my life, then one day my eyes were opened. I woke up one Sunday morning, as I was preparing myself for church. It all hit me. I said, now I see! Immediately, I was relieved of everything. The Almighty has a perfect way of working things out in our lives. Many things, we may not understand right off. Withal, we should still trust Him. He is in full control. *Job 21:3 "Suffer me that I may speak, and after that I have spoken, mock on." Job knew, beforehand how much he could trust our Heavenly Father.* No storm, trial or tribulation could confuse him. That is the purpose trials have for us; they cause us to be confused. During a terrible trial, you must know who your maker is to make it out. He simply knew. Job's tribulations were too great for the average person to experience and make it out on top. Perhaps, many would have lost their minds or apparently died because the grief would have been too much for them to bear. Job was strong. *Job 21:3, "Suffer me that I may speak; and after that I have spoken, mock on."* I

I can't take one more thing!

will never forget, one time in my life my neighbors thought I was crazy as many wondered, who is that woman? As they looked at me, they saw chaos all in my life. Friends were wondering, what is going on? Even some family began to whisper. My life was turned upside down and inside out. Everything was in a mess, including me. Whatever my hands touched, fell. So many nights I cried as I rocked myself to sleep. Often, I spoke to The Almighty and told Him this does not fare! I should not be going through all this. I know you can relate to times like these. I have praised you. I cannot take any more! You should not treat the ones you love this way. Jesus, stop this pain! No more, I can't take one more thing! Jesus, are you listening? Can you hear me? I cannot take one more thing; enough is enough! JESUS, JESUS, JESUS, help your daughter, I am dying! Why did I say that, because something else came? Every time I looked up, I began to face another crisis. Time after time, I had so much tribulation at once. I could not bear them all. A piece of me died here and there. Yes, the old me was dying. I will never be the same!" So many different

I can't take one more thing!

things were going on at once, I just could not take one more thing. The more I went through, the more the old me begin to pass away. *Job 23:10, "But He knoweth the way I take: when he hath tried me, I shall come forth as gold."* I remember how I use to let certain people use me, and eventually I stopped. That woman was dead. Some use to ride off my praise, because they did not have their own. I said, "no one else is going to suffocate my worship." I had friends that were not true to me. I let them go too. I woke up. I simply woke up! All of my aggravations were a wake-up call. I strategically learned a greater lesson out of everything I went through. Too many sleep too long before they realize many have used them dry to the bone. It is time, to wake up.

Never judge a book by its cover. You never know the truth behind the story, until you first read the book. *Matthew 7:1, "JUDGE NOT, that ye be not judged." We must stop judging people.* Maybe something terrible could have happened in their life. Perhaps, they are currently struggling just to hold on. You

I can't take one more thing!

never know what someone is going through just by looking at them. So many days, I wanted to bust out and cry. I could not. Often, I just needed someone to care. That very person could be going through the worst storm of their life. You never know! The Almighty might be using them and their situation to get your attention. I remember one Sunday at church before I was delivered. I saw this associate preacher, and I realized he was going to preach that particular Sunday. Of course, I did not want to hear him preach. I automatically judged him, no matter what I knew about him it was not my right to judge. Immediately, I felt as though The Almighty HIMSELF slapped me in my face. The voice of The Most High spoke to me and said, "as long as he is preaching and teaching my WORD, you listen!" My Word is food for your soul, the things he has done for me I will be the judge!" Since then, when I go to church the preacher's life is not my business. As The LORD leads me, I trust Him for a good word of encouragement. I refuse to let what someone else is not doing, cause me to miss out on a WORD of Life. Too many are walking more in

I can't take one more thing!

judgment, than in the WORD! Though The Holy Spirit shall righteously lead me to the place where I need to be, I learned not to judge, and I try not to. Is it worth allowing your flesh to cause you an opportunity of word instruction? I say if people want to play with the WORD, then that is on them. Regardless, I am going to receive what the WORD has for me. *Colossians 2:18, "Let no man beguile you of your reward in a voluntary humility and worshiping of angels, intruding into those things which he hath not seen, vainly puffed up by his fleshly mind."* Often, we have let others cause us to lose a blessing. Sometimes, people will work more against you, especially when they think you are going to outdo them. Satan knows a spiritual person that is why he attempts to destroy the good ones. No pain, no gain. The more you tried and overcame, is the more you will be strengthened. *Job 23:10, "But He knoweth the way I take: when he hath tried me, I shall come forth as gold."* Every time Satan tried Job, he was proved good. He showed Satan that he was faithful to The Almighty. How many demonstrate their faithfulness in distress by satisfying

I can't take one more thing!

God; not handling themselves well? That is when many will turn their backs on God. Job continued to prove to Satan just how loyal he was.

I know how hard it is to start over again and again. When you look ahead, all you can see is mountains the size of Mount Everest. It is too hard for you to climb. You are not in shape to make such an attempt. Being afraid at times and wondering if you might fall. Your mind is being fiddle, but guess what? There are no strings attached. The only thing in between you and that mountain is your faith. Your faith is what is going to get you to the top, not your climbing ability. When you look to your right, trouble is there. Road blocks are barricading you in and you cannot get through. Looking on your left, there are sinkholes in your pathway. They are too wide for you to go around and too deep to swim across. Often times, many people have begun to step backwards without noticing. All along movement has been taking place. Sometimes you panicked and were afraid of making a move forward. Often times being fearful will cause you to

I can't take one more thing!

make the wrong steps. *Acts 17:28 says, "For in him we live, and move, and have our being; as certain also of your own poets have said, For we are also his offspring."* Yes, that is exactly what Satan purposed for me to think, that I made the wrong move. No pain, no gain. Some things in life are purposed to be painful, so that you will never forget what you have overcome and who brought you through. Understand suffering is the best medicine to some. It will heal your wounds and give you time to rest and think. It will cause you to simply hear the voice of The Almighty and make you listen. Sometimes we tend to be so busy, we cannot hear the voice of The Almighty. I have to do this; I must go there. Every time you look around many are too occupied to spend time listening to our Heavenly Father. Well, Job was one that heard the voice of The Almighty. He was assured at all times.

Satan knows when you are in a stranded position in life. He knows when one is stuck in a sinkhole and wants to get out. As the wheels turn, they cannot be moved. He wants you to splash more assaults to cover

I can't take one more thing!

your life. So therefore, it will be impossible for one to move forward. Have you ever seen someone stuck in his or her vehicle along the side of the road? Notice, there tires are spinning and they are on ice. Perhaps, they are stuck in a mud puddle and cannot go anywhere. The wheels are just turning and spinning and making all types of noise and they are not getting anything done. As they press harder and harder on the gas peddle, still no movement. They are just wasting their time and yours. On top of that, they are in your way. Please get out of my way! You have a very important engagement, one that you cannot be late for or miss. Nevertheless, they are holding you and everyone around you back. Now they get out of their vehicle. You see them try to push the vehicle along, but it will not move. They try again and again. Everyone is noticing they need to call for help. That is another way the enemy attempts to stop us. He causes people and things to get in our way. He wants us to miss our opportunity of being blessed. Also, he wants us to be angry when others see us trying to move and they will not help. Satan wants us to turn around and

I can't take one more thing!

go another way. Yes, he tried that strategy with me. However, I'm one that will sit and wait. Often times, when we turn around we get stuck in another jam or held up anyhow. As I suffered, I had to mature by being patient. I realized, all the assaults and afflictions I experienced were teaching me to endure. It makes Him proud, when we simply do good. *Philippians 2:13, "For it is God which worketh in you both to will and to do of his good pleasure."*

Sometimes enduring a terrible trial can cause us not to be so good. Trials cause us to get angry, upset, be resentful, stressful, miserable, and so on. Enduring an extraneous trial is extremely difficult and yes, often times it is hard being good! *Job 3:1, "After this opened Job his mouth, and cursed his day."* Job too felt the aggravations of living life under pressure. He cursed the day he was born. Many of us have, when we too have filed our complaints with God. There are many forms of flesh from simple to big and often they are hidden. Surely, they come out during anger. When we get upset, it shows! It does not matter the form it

I can't take one more thing!

is, just repent. Sometimes God will let us linger in our terrible times, because of something so simple we have over looked. Flesh is very sizable and your terrible times can be too. Perhaps, Job could have been delivered sooner if he would not have resented his life. Understand, leave the complaints along and move forward with a clear mind. Be prepared to plunge in the depths of the power of Jesus. The more you talk about the past or that thing that has upset you the more you speak life to it. Stop, let it go and die! At times when things appear sour in your life, stop letting it spoil your joy. Find yourself some new hope in The Almighty. Surely, He has never let you down. Think back over your life, look at all Jesus has brought you through. Speak power to come in your life, simply say "Almighty forgive me for every wrong thing I have committed against you knowingly or not." Be sincere and ask Him to show you the way. During your trying times, you surely will find yourself. *Job 21:6, "Even when I remember I am afraid, and trembling taketh hold on my flesh."* No matter who we currently are in The Almighty, we all must live through fearful times.

I can't take one more thing!

It is all to try our faith and to expand our trust in Him. Actually, Jesus is just making our lives better. Yes, Job was a perfect man previously in the eyesight of The Most High. Not because of who he was but because of who The Almighty was making him to become. When The Most High was explaining Job to Satan, He was identifying Job as an overcomer. He knew that by the time Satan finished trying Job that he would come out being made to perfection. *(Hebrew 6:1)* Job had to endure very troubling times, just to make his loyalty appear perfect in the eyesight of Satan. *Ephesians 4:12, "For the perfecting of the saints, for the work of the ministry, for edifying of the body of Christ."* The Almighty needs many more to appear to Satan as Saints of The Most High, then this world would be a better place. We need to show others by being a living example, that we only grow tougher during our test and not weaker. However, every time The Almighty looks upon us, He sees our finishing. He sees us refined. He knows what we are going to have to go through, beforehand. Just remember, The Almighty is in control. In addition, when you finish

I can't take one more thing!

proving yourself to be good and faithful as you endure. You too, will be greatly rewarded. No pain, no gain!

Job 21:6, "Even when I remember I am afraid, and trembling taketh hold on my flesh." When the strongholds of your life are stronger than you, then you need the immediate strength you have never known. You need the strength of a Shield to protect you from the fiery darts of life. You need a mountain Rock, to cover you when the forces of the enemy are roaring against you and the Oil of your Butter to give you sliding ability. A King that can give you proper direction, lead you out of the pattern of destruction; also, a Shepherd to look after you when you are headed in harm's way. He is a Judge that will correct you when you are inconceivably wrong; a Refuge that will fight your battle during the times you give up. He has a Fortress of power that you can gain victorious strength of the highest capacity. He is an Avenger to avenge your death in the case of a wounded heart and He has the power to demolish any weapon that has

I can't take one more thing!

formed against you. Our Heavenly Father is a Creator that can speak anything into existence. He is someone that has the availability that will surely deliver you out of any situation because you believed without a shadow of a doubt against the enemy of confusion. He is a Miraculous Healer when the doctors tell you there is nothing that they can do, because He is the Savior of all the earth. He's a Protector from all hurt, harm, danger, and evil. He is a Provider of sufficiency, so that every need in your life will be bountifully met and met on time; and a Redeemer to awaken any dead thing within you, so that your soul will be granted the Eternal Life promised with pure happiness and peace. He is my Prince of Peace. He is Mercy forever more and full of Grace. In addition, Jesus is the truth, always showing me the way towards His marvelous Light.

I can't take one more thing!

Aggravated Assault On Your Mind

> *"I can't take one more thing.*
> *Enough is Enough!"*
> *~Parice C. Parker*

I can't take one more thing!

Aggravated Assault On Your Mind

CHAPTER 8
Stop The Aggravation

"You have the power to stop letting things and people aggravate you."

~ Parice C. Parker

I can't take one more thing!

CHAPTER 8

Stop The Aggravations

Systematically, to obtain your heart's desires, you must get persistent with your wants! Your faith must be activated. Overcoming is a spiritual system, and not everyone can tolerate their test. The only way is to The Almighty. You must grasp it with a pure heart determination until you seize what yours is. When you face the facts, and realize that enough is enough. You will begin to move forward with a perseverance that nothing or no one will get in your way. Enough is enough. You must make things happen, and be determined to conquer. Be a go getter and not a go-sitter. It will not matter what do not have; you will simply know that enough is enough. You will not be able to take another devastation in your life. You will, by all means necessary, do everything that is

I can't take one more thing!

in your power to push your faith to move. No longer will you consider what you need to make it because now you will be operating through The Supernatural. Simply saying, "It is now out of my hands, Jesus it is in yours." Regardless of what you need, you will begin to make things work. Your vision and ideas will become a rare moment, and nothing will stop your vision. Not even need! You will figure out a way when you can't take one more thing! Know that enough is enough. Believe all things are possible through Christ. Take control of every aspect of your life, by gaining intelligence through the WORD. Adopt the WORD of faith every day in your life and let it push you to fortune. *Philippians 4:6, "Be careful for nothing; but in everything by prayer and supplication with thanksgiving let your requests be made known unto God." Job 6:8, "Oh that I might have my request; and that God would grant me the thing that I longed for!"* Take your request to God. Be prepared to embrace every word that He has given you. Make it happen through gaining access to Heavenly Powers. When you begin to grasp the visual aspects of your request,

I can't take one more thing!

then you will receive favor from on high. *(11 Corinthians 2:9)* God's favor will make everything in your life come together, and totally line up with the word. It will create fruitfulness to overwhelm your life. This is the time; you must grasp the true hope of security. Always abide in HIM and Hold on to your faith. Your faith is what gets your request to The Almighty. Your faith is what gives you power. It will deliver any that are in need and speak life to the walking dead. Faith will allow you to move from one place to another. Your heart will lead you to the truth and no longer just a dream surrounded by clouds. When you give no attention to your assailants that have tried to assault your mind, then you will not feel the irritations of aggravations, that is when you think bad things are happening to you in your life. It will seem to bring more trouble. Instead of focusing on the worst, hold on to good. I always like to find one good reason or purpose out of every bad situation instead of letting thing during my eviction; I could not give into the problem of my eviction. I immediately gave The Almighty the praise for a brand new house. No matter

I can't take one more thing!

what I felt, God had covered my steps and ordered them. Though one door in my life closed, I knew, without a shadow of a doubt, that God was giving me the keys to my new home. I praised Him for a better home and received one. It was bigger and better than what I previously had. God is getting ready to bless you with bigger and better, just be patient.

Job 31:15, "Did not he that made me in the womb make him? and did not one fashion us in the womb?" So now is the time for you to stand stronger and in bigger faith in The Almighty. Quite naturally, if he did it for Job then he too will do the same for you. You must believe that The Almighty wants to give you bigger and better things that this world cannot offer you. He will give you things that money cannot buy and things not made by mans' hands. No matter what your eyes currently see, know that The Almighty is still in control. We search for many man-made reasons as to why this thing is happening. Still, no real answer. We are purposed to look for the unsearchable riches of our Heavenly Father. Put all your trust in The Almighty as Job did, that is why he received so much.

I can't take one more thing!

He knew The Almighty had all power; he knew God was still in charge of his life. Job realized that no matter what. He was covered by the Word of God and Job previously knew many that couldn't hold on, as they suffered. Job knew the consequences of not being patient. He also knew he could not do it by himself. It was only after the request he made to his Heavenly Father. Afterward, he was made whole again. Although it did not come overnight, it took time. Job could not stop proving himself to The Almighty, just because some things rose up in his life. He was not prepared to allow anything to separate or come in-between him and The Most High. The ONE that has always been there for him. Job knew it was nobody, but the Almighty that had previously blessed him. He was not willing to trust another to be God over his life. He too realized that there were many gods, but only one that was his! I believe that is why he made sure to call on the right one. He did not want a pagan god coming to his rescue. One thing I realized on my spiritual journey is that often we can speak the wrong things to happen in our lives. If you have a

I can't take one more thing!

complaining spirit, then you are making it your god. What if one has a lazy spirit, they too may lack and doubt their God. God is a spirit, and we must get an understanding of The Most High. Once one believes in The Most High, complaints will be far away! Things in one's life will transform from bad to good. Words create gods because what you speak comes into existence. If one speaks negative or trouble, it comes. When one speaks life, things begin to uplift. Perhaps, your words are causing downers and doubts, or uppers are causing prosperity to form in your life. Be careful of the things that come out of your mouth, because it is creating your future! So believe in the Spirit of The Most High and watch how He will raise you up! So, therefore, one day I wondered as Job was becoming tired, whom did he call on? I found out - The Almighty! He is the one that has all might. At that time, Jesus had not been born. Then I also wondered who did Adam & Abraham call. It was I AM. *Exodus 3:13 & 14 When Moses questions God, who shall I said me and asked me your name. And God said unto Moses, "I AM THAT I AM, I AM hath sent*

I can't take one more thing!

me." Too many times people tend to describe The Most High and it 's hard when I AM could be all things. I realized that I was not going to waste any more time in trying to figure all things out and begin working all things out in my life that is not producing. I AM everything that I am not. I AM everything I need. If I need a miracle healing, I AM is the HEALER. If I need a miraculous break through, I AM is the Master of BREAKTHROUGHS. If I need deliverance from anything, I AM is a DELIVERER. Whatever you need I AM is your need Supplier! He only produces life in abundance! Speaking, I AM the master of your needs, wants and heart's desires! He is your master, and I AM works through your faith. No one could supply your need greater than JESUS. It is by your FAITH that you shall be made whole. Not a day sooner, not a day later but your vision shall speak. Once your faith activates you NOW, I AM will produce!

In my mother's womb, I AM fashioned, and my future destined with righteousness. Though I had to go through, it was all for the glory of I AM to be

I can't take one more thing!

revealed. I have never noticed I AM to dress anyone to look a mess. You must believe everything that has occurred in your life, for the purpose of The Almighty to be evident through you. You are His walking evidence. In you is a wealthy inheritance and through your great substance shall be produced! When the devil wants to make you look a mess, show him what I AM can do. The Word strictly instructs us that if we seek The Kingdom of GOD (I AM) first, then all else will be added to our lives. It did not specify just a few things, but all things not excluding anything whatsoever. Only you have the ability to make your request known unto our Heavenly Father. Seek for The Kingdom of God (I AM). He will make all things happen for you and in your life. Diligently, seek Him because there is so much to learn of Him. We simply do not have time to rest on our journey; we must diligently seek Him. *Proverbs 10:4, "He becometh poor that dealeth with a slack hand: but the hand of the diligent maketh rich."* You are a wealth representative, and your life is speaking for The Kingdom. Imagine your children in the store looking a

I can't take one more thing!

hot mess with dirty shoes and dirty clothes. Someone may ask, "Where are your parents?" they point their finger at you. Noticing you look well dressed, how would it make you feel? Would it make you feel good about how they represent you? No. What would they see, when they catch you in a mess? Many in the Bible that overcame were more than conquers. As you seek Him, He will cause you to discover mysteries of how to be blessed in abundance. He wants to show others the adequate rewards of Kingdom mind setters! The more I seek for Him, the more I am taught of Him. *Proverbs 8:17, "I love them that love me; and those that seek me early shall find me."* The sooner you find Him, the sooner your request will be made known. He is the only one with all your needs. He has everything your heart ever desired, and He wants to give it to you. It is simple if you seek Him first. Seek His approval in everything you do and you will be righteously rewarded. God grants us privileges, blessings, power, and access through our faithfulness. Let Him add great things to your life. Then the scripture clearly states that He will add all things unto you. Being obedient

I can't take one more thing!

only subjects the power of The Almighty to be given unto you. He will be responsible for you. *Remember Matthew 6:33 "but seek ye first the kingdom of GOD, and His righteousness and all these things shall be added unto you."* Once you realize the importance of giving The Almighty your undivided attention, your mind will remain in Him and His Word. He will begin to create things that you never thought were possible, from material to Wisdom. So many believers cause their aggravations. They ask The Almighty for a special request, but they quit seeking Him on their journey towards it. Also, some cannot handle how he delivers it to them. The same way you gain is the same spiritual strategy you must keep obtaining. Just keep putting Him first. *II Corinthians 1:9, "But we had the sentence of death in ourselves, that we should not trust in ourselves but in God, which raiseth the dead:"*

What if Job would have begun to trust himself, vice versa the Word of the Almighty. He would have never made it out alive. Often we lose ourselves during the struggles of life. Continue seeking after righteousness, do not trust anything or

I can't take one more thing!

any other God. I once knew this person as they begin to trust their friends. The more they stop feeding themselves righteousness, the more Satan enjoyed himself in their life. This person was brutally attacked. This person was getting beat so bad until they hardly fought back. I tried to help, but they did not want to receive it. As I looked at the individual, I began to pray more. I start to run faster to safety. I also kept the Word growing in my life, by keeping it nearer. The worst thing in life is when you cannot hear The Almighty. I felt for this individual, because as I saw them critically suffer. I said, "All they need is to call on JESUS!" In most cases, many make their situation worse, because they stop putting God first. There is absolutely no greater trust on the face of this earth to invest in, other than The Almighty. Jesus is the way maker, and He is powerful. *(Matthew 28:18, "And Jesus came and spake unto them, saying, All power is given unto me in heaven and earth.")* No matter what you need, He will go and make the way so you can obtain it. If you do not ask, then how will you ever receive? Seeking is an action word, just like faith. It

I can't take one more thing!

searches when you search, and it finds what it seeks. If you never take a decision on your request, then how can you truly receive it? Your faith will get you there, but faith without works are dead.

Job 31:2, "For what portion of God is there from above? and what inheritance of the Almighty from on high?" Sometimes you will look at others like you are in desperate need. Or perhaps, without the ability to carry on. Those same people that talked about you scandalized your name and tried to put your name to shame. One day The Almighty is going to use it all, for a token of His good. *(Psalms 86:17)* He will show others, who they went against. Also, those that were your enemies, The Almighty will make them be your footstool. During your faith-building process, be steadfast and unmovable. At all times, look through your spiritual eyes. You will make it. Job was determined to overcome. Through his sickness, his mind was made up. After all, he lost; his mind was made up to wait patiently on The Lord. Maybe, Job remembered how he was there for others during their time of need. One that blesses those that are less

I can't take one more thing!

fortunate always has a higher power to look up. *Psalms 41: 1, "Blessed is he that considereth the poor: the LORD will deliver him in time of troubles."* Job believed in the Almighty; He knew his portion of deliverance. Job blessed many people, and his life was dedicated to being a blessing. He was aware that The Almighty would protect him, during his times of need. *Psalms 41:2, "The LORD will preserve him, and keep him alive; and he shall be blessed upon the earth: and thou wilt not deliver him unto the will of his enemies."*

Sometimes as we go through tough times, many tend to appear blameless. Often I looked back over my life and many times, I could not understand why the enemy was assaulting me. My response, I too had not been what I needed to be. It could be something such as growing in patience; understanding faith has a mighty way of operating on you. The enemy in most cases wants us frustrated as to why we are being tried. Also, we overlook something so simple and innocent. Such as patience being highly developed to formulate us to a particular faith. The one that pleases The Most High. Job had faith that

I can't take one more thing!

ultimately pleased The Almighty and all that Job endured completed The Most High in him. Afterward, his faith possessed divine substance, double for his trouble!

As I spiritually matured I realized, it was not easy. Honestly, if it had not been for me holding on to The WORD. I would have lost my mind. If I had not knelt down to pray, I would have gone crazy. If I had not tuned into The Holy Spirit, I would have not survived. *Job 31:6, "Let me be weighed in an even balance, that God may know my integrity."* Though we must endure life assaults, we have to allow them to strengthen us in areas where we are weak. Integrity is when you hear the I AM in you and know that you must maintain a supernatural ability to be incorruptible. You must grow to a certain faith that nothing can intercept your spiritual manifestation. Being incorruptible is the integrity God requires of the ones that please Him. Regardless of what one is going through, he still will promote the KINGDOM, no matter what state your life is. The incorruptible always walk by faith, and they never see with their natural

I can't take one more thing!

eyes. Once the pure faith is birthed through you, no one would ever be able to persuade you of another God. Neither would they be able to take you away from Jesus. Your life shall speak and persuade them, that He is at large in you. Sooner than later, they would have to inquire on whom you serve. You too can tell them, I AM!

I too thought I was strong enough in The Almighty until I begin to go through my greatest trial. It was life threatening. Job knew who he was beforehand. Afterward, I can imagine. WOW! The average person would have given up and rolled over as well as died. However, Job grew in patience because He knew what he was before he was finished! Wow! What an effect being patient will have in your life. *Job 31:6, "Let me be weighed in an even balance, that God may know my integrity."* After all Job went through he was evenly balanced. Perhaps, the same is happening to you. He is balancing out the fruit of His spirit in you. One thing I realized is that the Almighty wants us evenly balanced. As we are being developed with integrity, we must be evenly balanced. Not too

I can't take one more thing!

much of this and in the need of that. Job was highly developed until his integrity was complete. Our Heavenly Father wants all the ruins to be removed out of our lives. Understand the way He is developing me may not be the way He causes you to be remade. Perhaps, the greatest key to this story is that when God was looking at Job, he was looking into His future once He finished him. When God puts His eyes on something, He can see the good and know the value. Probably, that could have been the reason God looked upon Job as pleasing unto His eyesight. However, He knew how perfect Job was going to come out once He finished developing Job's integrity. After all, his integrity began to show how much he valued The Most High. If you be loyal to Jesus, He must return the favor from The Most High to be loyal to you.

Job 21:6, "Even when I remember I am afraid, and trembling taketh hold on my flesh." When the strongholds of your life are stronger than you, then you need the immediate strength you have never known. You need the strength of a Shield to protect you from the fiery darts of life. You need a mountain

I can't take one more thing!

Rock, to cover you when the forces of the enemy are roaring against you and the Oil of your Butter to give you sliding ability. A King that can give you perfect direction, lead you out of the pattern of destruction; also, a Shepherd to look after you when you are headed in harm's way. He is a Judge that will correct you when you are inconceivably wrong; a Refuge that will fight your battle during the times you give up. He has a Fortress of power that you can gain victorious strength, of the highest capacity. An Avenger to avenge your death in the case of a wounded heart and He has the power to demolish any weapon that has formed against you. Our Heavenly Father is a Creator that can speak anything into existence. Miraculous Healer - when the doctors tell you there is nothing that they can do, because He is the Savior of all the earth. A Protector from all hurt, harm, danger, and evil. He is a Provider of sufficiency so that every need in your life will be bountifully met and met on time. A Redeemer to awaken any dead thing within you, so that your soul will be granted the Eternal Life promised with pure happiness and peace. He is my

I can't take one more thing!

Prince of Peace. He is Mercy forever more and full of Grace. Also, Jesus is the truth, always showing me the way towards His marvelous Light.

I can't take one more thing!

Aggravated Assault On Your Mind

"Stop Hiding Your Value and Throw Whatever Is Holding You Back Overboard!"

~Parice C. Parker

I can't take one more thing!

Aggravated Assault On Your Mind

CHAPTER 9
Throw Some Stuff Overboard

"When you get rid of some stuff, watch how far you will get!"

~ Parice C. Parker

I can't take one more thing!

CHAPTER 9

Throw Some Stuff Overboard

The Almighty instructed Jonah to go to Nineveh, the great city and warn them of their wickedness. Jonah thought he could run away from obeying The Almighty, and he fled to Tarshish. The Almighty spoke to Jonah and commissioned him. He also instructed him where to go. I know our Heavenly Father speaks to all, some obey and others are disobedient. He gives many instructions, but many feel incompetent. Perhaps, Jonah feared because he was not strong enough. Alternatively, he did not have everything he needed to see his way. God never intends for us to worry about what we do not have. He wants us to operate in obedience. *Jonah 1:3, "Arise, go to Nineveh, that great city, and cry against it; for their wickedness is come before me."* He did what he

I can't take one more thing!

wanted and disregarded God. Therefore, he found a ship in Joppa that was going to Tarshish and paid the fare. *(Jonah 1:3)* Reminds us the price we will pay for being disobedient. It is a hefty and dangerous price. The cost of being disobedient is extremely expensive and wasteful. It is the prime reason many lives tormented for so long with aggravations. I have seen big dreams go down the drain because someone ran away from the instruction of The LORD. Homes have foreclosed, businesses shut down, families separated, children gone astray, many have gone to prison, some in foster care and quite a few are six feet under. It is not worth being disobedient to the instructions of The LORD. Who's depending on you, before their deliverance can take place? Notice, you only view the ones in mind that you know, but what about those that you do not know? We all have more than we could think of who are in need of deliverance. Assaults on your mind can only afflict a mind not made up. Jonah realized he was disobedient to the direction of The Almighty. More than enough times, many paid to double the price to live in their mess. I call it cruel and

I can't take one more thing!

unusual punishment with a jacked up interest rate. A lot of people are wasting valuable time that could have added to an escrow account of blessings. Nevertheless, because they had no interest in hearing instruction from the voice of the Almighty, He could not give attention to their heart's desires. Jonah had planned to run from God. However, still in the midst, The Almighty was revealing Himself to Jonah. So, therefore, after the ship had begun to sail God allowed high winds to come forth. *(Jonah 1:4) It up roared the sea, causing the ship to sail into dangerous waters.* Everyone aboard the ship was afraid and wondered why and who was causing this danger to come. It was an excellent example of how one person can cause an uproar in your life due to their disobedience to God. *(Jonah 1:5) The Mariners asked everyone to pray, to lighten the roaring of the sea. The Almighty has a fine way to warn us to be careful in our lives.* Jonah was the very person running from the Almighty and the last to pray. He brought all that trouble on the ship with him because he was running away from God. However, Jonah laid there sleeping as though nothing

I can't take one more thing!

was happening. They went over to awake Jonah and told him to pray. Jonah was being very selfish while others were praying; He knew why the storm was roaring, but he did not care. Sometimes people come into our lives and do not care about us. As long as he was riding, he did not care that others were fearful. He probably did not want to suffer alone. Selfish people want others to fall with them. They do not go down by themselves or ride in a storm lonely. Soon the Mariners cast lots, and it fell upon Jonah. They asked Jonah, what was his business on their ship? They wanted to know who he was. They begin to question Jonah. Where did you come from, and who are you? It is so important who and why you connect to a person or individual. Look at the trouble Jonah brought with him. It was deep, and they begin to search for answers. They wanted to know whom Jonah knew on the ship. Look over your life. At times, certain people can and will bring terrible storms with them. If you connect with them, you will feel the shifting of the storm. It will soon affect your life. One thing about a storm, it does not care who is around. It will not stop until it is

I can't take one more thing!

over. You would be forced to ride it out if you want to survive or die in your storm. They knew it could only be Jonah, because before he had gotten there everything was all right. Jonah immediately let the shipmates know he was troubled, because of his disobedience to God. The men drew exceedingly afraid of Jonah, for now, they knew it was something evil about him. When you do not listen to God, you will cause yourself a life of troubles. You will lose your ability to stay focused on where you are going. Nevertheless, you will pay more for your troubles. The instructions of the LORD are extremely vital. After all, why continue causing the storms to affect all that is around you? Jonah was being very selfish, and he did not care who was suffering with him. Sometimes, we have that same kind of people in our lives. They see you going down, and they know the reason, and they are too stubborn to get out of your life. They know they are only riding off your blessings and favor from the Almighty that is connected with you. Their desires are not what God wanted for their lives, and because of it more suffer due to their

I can't take one more thing!

disobedience. It is a hurting thing when others see you suffer, because of their foolishness. Always remember, if they do not care about you then it is not your business to continue suffering for their selfishness.

It is aggravating when one selfish person will cause the whole crew to suffer. *1 Timothy 6:5, "Perverse disputings of men of corrupt minds, and destitute of the truth, supposing that gain is godliness: from such withdraw thyself."* Stay watchful at all times. Keep your eyes open and look ahead. Some chaos will form in your life, only because you connect to the wrong person(s). It is time to throw some stuff on board and out of your life. Some things we do not have to go through, we just need to open our eyes and check our company. The scariest kind of person to deal with is the one that is running from God. *1 Timothy 6:5, "Perverse disputings of men of corrupt minds, and destitute of the truth supposing that gain is godliness: from such withdraw thyself."*

I am speaking of those that will learn from the world, but lose spiritual interest in Jesus. It is scary

I can't take one more thing!

because they do not care. If one does not care about The Almighty, why should they care about you? Once I was going through an expensive experience in my life, some people almost caused me to drown. I woke up and begin to throw some stuff on board. Some things will weigh you down in your life. People will burden you, and you need to throw it and them overboard. Jesus wants some things and some people out of your life. He wants you to do what is necessary to withdraw yourself. There is no use for the both of you drowning. Some people just do not wish to be saved! It is time to protect yourself!

I will never forget the many people I had in my life. Some I loved and enjoyed spending time with, but Jesus no longer wanted me to socialize with them. They weighed me down. When you associate with people that make you do foolish things, you must leave them alone. It seemed like every time I thought I was moving ahead, something always crumbled down. It was the burdens I was faced with and one day I woke up. I realized that some of them were taking me for granted. They were using me, as some will say,

I can't take one more thing!

"for a free ride." I know it sounds awkward, but it is true. I found out how many people will use you, especially when they know you are a believer. One day it hit me. The Holy Spirit said, "You have a destination, and you cannot get there with all this extra baggage." As The Almighty was leading me towards the promise land, I was still carrying too much weight. I had to throw even more stuff overboard. Many will try you as they play games. It is not worth it. Some relationships can begin to be too costly. People will use you, only if you let them. Before you know it, you will be broken down and without anything. Some will cost you your inheritance, family, career, vision and righteousness. However, it is time to throw some stuff and people overboard. When the Holy Spirit tells you to withdraw yourself, do not hesitate. Not everyone is headed in the same direction as you. Regardless of their talk, you have to start noticing their walk. I refuse to allow a heavy burden to destroy me, whether it is a thing or a person. If you try to weigh me down, I must throw you overboard. I refuse to let my life sink, because of others' unexpected baggage. It can

I can't take one more thing!

aggravate your life and will cause you to fall, as well as drown. Just as these shipmates were serious, I was too. Get serious about your life. Jesus does not expect you to ride through a storm that is meant for someone else. I tell people if you do not want to straighten up, then do not try to mess me up. Also, if you do not wish to get anywhere in your life. Do not attempt to slow me down. Some people I realized, loved trouble. I have a purpose in my life, and that is to overcome. These shipmates were determined to get back on course. They had a destination point, and they were not going to let Jonah hold them back. Most assuredly, they were not ready to drown because they had too much to look forward too, their payday. A job isn't complete until it is done and they were prepared to finish their course.

When The Almighty gives instructions, listen. After the shipmates had realized that Jonah was the sufficient cause of the raging sea, they began to pray. They recognized God had the power to stop their storm from raging. They sought The Almighty through communicating with Him. They prayed that God

I can't take one more thing!

would not to let them perish, because of Jonah's disobedience. After they had prayed, they agreed to throw Jonah overboard into the raging waters. However, the Almighty clearly saw the seriousness of the shipmates throw Jonah overboard. Our Heavenly Father had to place a whale in the sea, large enough to catch Jonah. He allowed a great fish to swallow him, so Jonah would not drown.

These shipmates had a destination, and they were determined to make it there. They were not going to allow some form of an evil spirit to hinder their progress or cause them to drown. Many of us need to be like these shipmates. People need to protect their ground and their crew. Especially when you know something is out of order. Some people truly carry their problems with them. They are so big until they cause everyone around them danger. You must be aware whom and what is in your surroundings. *Jonah 1:13, "Nevertheless the men rowed hard to bring it to the land; but they could not: for the sea wrought, and was tempestuous against them."* Admittedly, they attempted to get the ship out of harm's way, but as

I can't take one more thing!

long as Jonah was on board the sea raged. After they put in a full effort to save everyone, they sought the advice of the LORD. *(Jonah 1:13-16)*. The shipmates came in agreement, prayed in unity and then threw Jonah overboard. Once they forced their prayer power together, they all stood on the same agreement in The Spirit of God. Jonah had to go! Sometimes you have to think in the same perspective. Someone or some things just have to go. They were determined to make it to their destination, and they were not afraid of what was going to happen to Jonah. They threw him overboard. The shipmates' minds were made up, they were going to finish their journey, and they wanted to get back on course. Sometimes we care too much for others that we just do not take the time to care about us. If someone cared about you in the manner you cared about them, then the rage would not have begun. The sea raged because they had the wrong person onboard. When difficulties come in your life, you need to look at whom you have on board in your life. Sometimes, we allow the storms to rage in our lives, because of someone else's disobedience towards God.

I can't take one more thing!

Are you determined enough to make it to your destination point? If so, then get rid of whatever is holding you back. People will hold you back, only if you let them. Who you have in your life, are the choices you have made. They will mess up your life and then cause you to drown. I say if people want to play with their lives, and then let them. However, do not let them play with yours. I can get anything material thing replaced in my life, but I only have one life opportunity! I decided to make the best of it. Everyone that is not of The Almighty or walking in agreement in my life must go. Some things you have to throw overboard. *Jonah 1:14, "Wherefore they cried unto the Lord, and said, we beseech thee, let us not perish for this man's life, and lay not upon us innocent blood: for thou, O Lord, hast done as it pleased thee."*

What if these men had not pleased The Almighty? Possibly the whole ship would have drowned. The Holy Spirit gives us instructions, and He expects us to follow. Look around, whose life is connected to yours? These men had to throw Jonah

I can't take one more thing!

overboard; they prayed on his behalf as well. Once you pray for the ones you cannot help, then leave them in Jesus' hands. He will take care of them. Now, in the meantime, get back on course. You may not like the instructions He gives you, but you must follow them.

No matter how you look at life, you cannot survive anything without faith. You will have faith that you can, or that you can't. Either way, it will be one or the other. So, why not believe that you can? You will be amazed how faith and obedience operate as one. Together, they are extremely powerful. What if Jonah would have had enough faith to obey the voice of The LORD at first? Most assuredly, he had enough not to fear him and see where that got him. So, therefore, put your faith in the positive and your results will always be good. *Acts 3:16, "And his name through faith in his name hath made this man strong, whom ye see and know: Yea, the faith which is by him hath given him this perfect soundness in the presence of you all."* These shipmates were determined to believe in the powers of The Almighty to deliver them, and He did. They depended on God to stop the waters from raging,

I can't take one more thing!

and He did. They called on Him, and He appeared in time. *Jonah 1:13, "Nevertheless the men rowed hard to bring it to the land; but they could not: for the sea wrought, and was tempestuous against them."* Your life can take a turn for the right course if you call upon The LORD and obey Him. On the other hand, once you remove yourself from some people that are not obeying the voice of the LORD. The Almighty will deliver you in the nick of time, and He will stop your raging sea. You can either decide if you want to live or die; it is your life. Trying to save everyone around you is not the key, save yourself. Once you are saved, then others will be able to call upon The LORD. Your life will reflect how powerful He is. Someone must lead, for someone else to follow. The Almighty is calling you to lead. Listen, you cannot concern yourself trying to save others that do not want to be saved. Only Jesus has the power to save anyone. However, the ones that want to be saved will call upon Him for themselves. *Jonah 1:15 says, "So they took up Jonah, and cast him forth into the sea: and the sea ceased from her rage."* Jonah's disobedience caused Him to be shut up

I can't take one more thing!

in the belly of hell. When God has a plan for your life, no matter what you do or where you run, His plan will go forth. Now, what if Jonah would not have entrusted the shipmates with the truth. Surely, they all could have drowned. During this incident, these shipmates had the opportunity of being saved through the power of The Almighty. Never underestimate how our Heavenly Father works, or whom He uses to get the job done. He is known for making the disobedient obey Him one way or another. Listening to the voice of The LORD can be either hard or easy. Which would you prefer?

The sooner we obey Him, the sooner we will be delivered. *Jonah 2:2, "And said, I cried because of mine affliction unto the Lord, and he heard me; out of the belly of hell cried me and thou heardest my voice."* Jonah was locked up in the belly of hell, but God had mercy on Him. Our Heavenly Father's mercy is unlimited, and Jonah still needed His mercy. It does not matter where you are, and God can supply you mercy. *(Psalms 136)* Do not allow your hellhole to stop you from crying out to God. He will have mercy

I can't take one more thing!

on you. His mercy can reach anyone and anywhere. He has unlimited stretching ability. Let His mercy deliver you out of your Belly of Hell.

What if the shipmates would not have thrown Jonah overboard? He would not have had the opportunity of getting correct with The Almighty. Perhaps, they would have interfered with the work of The Lord. However, they would have complied with Jonah's disobedience. Simply saying, they would have been working against The LORD. Often, we have interfered with the work of The Almighty. Sometimes we allow ourselves to be in a lock down position by our Heavenly Father. Do not interfere, when God is working on someone, let God be The Almighty over their life and not you. Jonah 9:1 says, But I will sacrifice unto thee with the voice of thanksgiving; I will pay that I have vowed. Salvation was of The Lord. *(Jonah 1:16) When Jonah made a promise to The LORD; he was delivered! Psalms 50:14-15, "Offer unto God thanksgiving, and pay thy vows unto The Most High. (15) And call upon me in the day of trouble: I will deliver thee, and thou shalt glorify me."*

I can't take one more thing!

Many do not understand the purpose of the vow. It is an act of our Heavenly Father to perform greater in your life. Once your promise is complete, you inherit. The WORD guarantees you His trust. Never take vowing for granted, it is extremely powerful. It has the power to deliver you from the depths of hell. His WORD is true. Whatever you need, obey Him and see with your own two eyes how He will bring it all to pass. It is supernatural performance power. Because once you complete your vow, The Almighty performs your miracle. Jonah pledged to achieve what he said he would do for God. *Jonah 2:9 says, But I will sacrifice unto thee with thanksgiving; I will pay that that I have vowed. Salvation is of The LORD.* That is what got him out of the belly of hell. Complete your vow to The Lord and let it perform. Surely, it will bond you closer to Him. Jonah wanted to give The Almighty what He wanted. Jonah wanted to come out. Our Heavenly Father can use you anytime you are ready, just give Him your word. *Jonah 2:1, "Then Jonah prayed unto the Lord his God out of the fish's belly."* He wants you to open your heart and pour out

I can't take one more thing!

right where you are. Notice, if one can see Him in their belly of hell; then they have all possibilities of deliverance. His presence is powerful, and His WORD is life. It does not matter what hell you are living. All that matters is that once you call upon His name, you will be delivered. The thought alone of calling upon Jesus will cause you to begin to be set free. Though Jonah was in the belly of a fish, God had a way of delivering Him. The Almighty can hear you anywhere. No amount of hell should hold you back from what our Heavenly Father has purposed for your life. He requires greatness out of you. Want your miracle, give Him a miracle and obey! What The Almighty has been a purpose for your life, it shall be done.

Another life aggravation that many tend to bring upon themselves is turning a deaf ear towards The Almighty. The Holy Spirit speaks to us, and always releases power to grant life, whether it is to us or someone else. Many times, we are so busy looking at our own messed up lives that we think we cannot handle the task our Heavenly Father has given us. We would rather save our selfish lives, instead of many

I can't take one more thing!

others benefiting greater. The Almighty needed Jonah to preach life to a dying city, but he fled because of fear. *Jonah 3:2, "Arise, go unto Nineveh, that great city, and preach unto it the preaching that I bid thee."* This is not the time for anyone to fear Him because there is power in obedience. *Proverbs 21:3, "To do justice and judgment is more acceptable to the Lord than sacrifice."* Our Heavenly Father wants us to do what is right. The more we listen to Him, the better life we all will live. Also, the less trouble we would have to deal with. Listen when He speaks.

Being disobedient to the voice of The LORD will make us experience trauma in life we should never have to experience. Yes, it will cause us some form of hell. Jonah was locked up in the belly of hell, due to his disobedience. Eventually, he recognized how dangerous the voice of God was. Jesus wants to stop the rage in your life, but there are some things you need to throw over board. However, the sea may rage. Jesus can cause it all to cease. I do not know what those things are in your life. However, you do. It is time to get rid of the things and people that keep the

I can't take one more thing!

rage brewing in your life. Soon as you throw them overboard, The Almighty will rid your life of all rage. Your life will then become smooth sailing. It will be peaceful and great. You will get to where you are going sooner because the extra baggage will not be hindering you. Lighten your load and cruise on into a glorious peaceful life. Imagine if Jonah had kept on running, he probably would have soon died in the Belly of Hell. *Psalms 19:14, "Let the words of my mouth, and the meditation of my heart, be acceptable in thy sight, O LORD, my strength, and my redeemer."* The key to becoming free is to run to Jesus instead of away.

Job 21:6, "Even when I remember I am afraid and trembling hold of my flesh." When the strongholds of your life are stronger than you, then you need the immediate strength you have never known. You need the strength of a Shield to protect you from the fiery darts of life. You need a mountain Rock, to cover you when the forces of the enemy are roaring against you and the Oil of your Butter to give you sliding ability. A King that can give you perfect

I can't take one more thing!

direction, lead you out of the pattern of destruction; also, a Shepherd to look after you when you are headed in harm's way. He is a Judge that will correct you when you are inconceivably wrong; a Refuge that will fight your battle during the times you give up. He has a Fortress of power that you can gain victorious strength of the highest capacity. He is an Avenger to avenge your death in the case of a wounded heart, and He has the power to demolish any weapon that has formed against you. Our Heavenly Father is a Creator that can speak anything into existence. He is someone that has the availability that will surely deliver you out of any situation because you believed without a shadow of doubt against the enemy of confusion. He is a Miraculous Healer when the doctors tell you there is nothing that they can do because He is the Savior of all the earth. He's a Protector from all hurt, harm, danger, and evil. He is a Provider of sufficiency so that every need in your life will be bountifully met and met on time, and a Redeemer to awaken any dead thing within you so that your soul will grant the Eternal Life promised with pure happiness and peace.

I can't take one more thing!

He is my Prince of Peace. He is Mercy forever more and full of Grace. Also, Jesus is the truth, always showing me the way towards His marvelous Light.

I can't take one more thing!

Aggravated Assault On Your Mind

"Be Unbeatable!"

~Parice C. Parker

I can't take one more thing!

Aggravated Assault On Your Mind

CHAPTER 10
No Weapon Formed

"Nothing shall hurt or harm you, it's all to make you become unbeatable!"

~ Parice C. Parker

I can't take one more thing!
CHAPTER 10

No Weapon Formed

When trying times come in your life, it is a sign that spiritual maturity needs to take place. You have to grow up in the WORD. Most times you will have to develop fast. The greater your suffering is, the more you grow. How can you handle a great trial, if you cannot expand your strength to become a great warrior? Regardless, the trial will get the best of you, or you will get the best out of it. The little trials prepare one for a little expansion. However, the great trials, make one to become unbeatable. You grow as your experiments teach you valuable lessons. Look back over your life and notice that every trial left a mark. It was either right or wrong, big or small. However, you learned an actual valuable lesson on the do's and dont's. Simply saying you gained more

I can't take one more thing!

wisdom. The harder the trial, the greater your victory. Begin to get personal with your trial and introduce your trial to your Maker! *Romans 8:18 "For I reckon that the sufferings of this present time are not worthy to be compared with the glory which shall be revealed in us."* Let every enemy know that no weapon shall form against you shall prosper when you become determined to overcome. Nevertheless, if it had not been for trials, then how would one become such a great warrior? I allowed my trials to become a growth spurt of faith. I just simply refused to let anyone abuse me or anything make me appear less than my worth. For years I surrounded myself with people that disrespected The Anointing God had developed in me. One evening I changed, and my future immediately begin to look brighter. Why, because I decided to respect what God required of me. *Isaiah 54:17 "No weapon that is formed against thee shall prosper; and every tongue that shall rise against thee in judgment thou shall condemn. This is the heritage of the servants of the Lord, and their righteousness is of me, saith the Lord."* Often, we tend to weaken because of

I can't take one more thing!

others' needs. We allow them to drain The Anointing out of us, simply because we want to hold on. When The Almighty begins to remove things and people out of your life, let it be! Do not try to hold someone near, because you do not want to lose them or see them leave. Weapons live through people because they move spiritually. Learn how to act in obedience and hear The Almighty when He tells you to rid yourself of the wrong relationships, things and living conditions. Disfigure the weapon of destruction in those that do not respect you, by closing the door. It is time to move on, so you can move forward! Turn your heart breaks and heartaches into a form of prosperity! Become unbeatable! The tables seemed to have turned around, just hold onto whatever The Almighty told you. He will bring it all to past, every heartache, every troubled time and every terrible thing that has happened in your life. Believe, if you hang on just a little while longer it all will be well worth it. Only you know what The Almighty has told you and only you can hold on to His voice. His words to you shall not go void. So therefore, immediately give The Most High

I can't take one more thing!

the praise for your tremendous victory. You do not serve an ordinary GOD, but The Almighty that is the creator of all and everything. Daily, God breaths upon the face of this earth and gives new life. The Almighty you serve loves to bless. The many impossible defeats that will constantly arise in your life, will cause you to be unbeatable. When you realize that you can operate in His supreme authority, then you will begin to change. He is your defense and, The Holy Spirit is your power. No longer let the enemy steal your joy, or kill your faith and rob your hope from The Almighty.

For the enemy can take absolutely nothing that you do not give him. The Almighty is our Alpha & Omega. When The Almighty created you, He had already blessed you from your mother's womb and predestined His will for your life. The life one lives has all possibilities to be great. Right now, prophesy no more! Absolutely, no more can the enemy have, take or destroy anything else that The Almighty has purposed for you. Remember, whatever The Almighty blesses you with, then no man on the face of this earth can take it away. I AM has complete control over this

I can't take one more thing!

particular weapon that has formed against you. Just think of what kind of GOD you serve. The Almighty has already worked out miracles beyond miracles within your life. You know that many of your prayers have already answered, repeatedly! Just imagine the times before you did not give up hope, but continued through it all. Regardless of your situation, The Almighty is still there. No weapon can form against you without God's authorization. I do not feel within my heart that GOD is going to assign a weapon to destroy you. The Almighty is not the God of destruction, but the GOD of creation. *Isaiah 54:17 "No weapon that is formed against thee shall prosper; and every tongue that shall rise against thee in judgment thou shall condemn.* This is the heritage of the servants of the Lord, and their righteousness is of me, saith the Lord." Though it seems the weapon has been tearing at your capacity to cause you to give up, this moment in your life may irritate you and cause you to be aggravated. GOD intends you to be strengthened to a point in HIM that no man or enemy can take you away. Maybe through a weapon that has

I can't take one more thing!

formed will cause a transformation through the Spirit of The Most High to bring about a change for the good. Remember, whatever the enemy means for your bad, The Almighty is turning your situation around for your good. Regardless of the pressures rising in you, just put your trust in The Almighty and He will bless you again. It is totally up to your faith to overcome this weapon of destruction if you want victory? Then be victorious! I know that The Most High is going to keep His word, even when we do not keep ours. *Isaiah 54:17 "No weapon that is formed against thee shall prosper; and every tongue that shall rise against thee in judgment thou shall condemn.* This is the heritage of the servants of the Lord, and their righteousness is of me, saith the Lord." Occasionally, we may feel fatigue in the way we hope, but the way we exercise our faith is the greater. The Almighty can be God in our lives. You may feel that you cannot lift this load; well guess what? It is not for you to lift. That is the number one reason a lot of folks' burdens turn into lifelong problems because they cannot handle it! *John 14:1 "Let not your heart be troubled: ye believe*

I can't take one more thing!

in God, believe also in me." Jesus knows you cannot carry the load, but He can! He knows exactly how much we can bear and how much of a load we can carry. That is why we have to exercise our faith in Him. Remember, no matter what you are going through, do not let it assault your mind to hinder your trust in Jesus. *Isaiah 54:17 "No weapon that is formed against thee shall prosper; and every tongue that shall rise against thee in judgment thou shall condemn. This is the heritage of the servants of the Lord, and their righteousness is of me," saith the Lord.*

Getting a grip on reality, and grasping that moment of aggravation. Now, it is time to let it go! Stop holding onto the things of life that you have no control! Release it immediately in the name of JESUS! Leave it to The Almighty and think of it no more. This is not the time to question your faith if GOD is going to answer you or even if He is going to help you. Just give it to Him. *Isaiah 54:1 "No weapon that is formed against thee shall prosper; and every tongue that shall rise against thee in judgment thou shall condemn. This*

I can't take one more thing!

is the heritage of the servants of the Lord, and their righteousness is of me," saith the Lord.

Because of fear the enemy attacks the minds and hinders one's progress. The Almighty's will is for things in our lives to be a smooth operation and flowing with righteous favor from The Most High. Many are holding back on GOD, fearing the moment of change. Often times many allow the enemy to put forth the accusation of assaults, because of the mistakes of others. I blamed churches, so-called friends, word believers, and even family members. Truly, it was my entire fault. I just wanted to make a difference in some dying woman, boy, girl or daddy's life; by presenting my cause. Surely, I was trying too hard of self and not enough of Him. Many have the right heart motivation, to want to make the right moves and trying to make the right change. Nevertheless, many put the blame on another giving excuses of things going wrong in their lives. For years I stayed at a standstill position, because I was not working my faith. I put the blame on everyone but me. No one is to blame for your life. Surely, some things

I can't take one more thing!

you did not have full control over and others you made a conscious decision. Stop trying to figure out who's to blame and begin to look at self. In addition, often people try to outdo themselves by helping others. However, they could hardly help themselves. Make sure you take a closer look at the decisions you make, so that unnecessary burdens would not become heavy loads.

One day, I will never forget, I really had screwed things up in my life, because I was always putting the needs of others first. I was trying to make everything better for others and all along I was neglecting me. It is a trip being concerned about people that do not respect or care if you are still living. I bent over backwards for a lot of people that literally did not care. One day as I took a deeper look at me. I realized it was no one's fault, but mine. Here I was trying to help others, and could hardly help myself! If one allow others to continue to mistreat them, then it is no one's fault but theirs. Many things can end just as they begin. It only takes a second of your life, to make up your mind that enough is enough! Allow The Most

I can't take one more thing!

High to have true authority over your life. Notice, life is only mind over matter. Surely, The Almighty's will is far greater than ours. So therefore His power of authorization matters, more than ours.

A will is something that is not forceful, but in the spirit is willing. One must be willing to live free and clear. Have you ever liked anyone or thing that was forceful with you? I can imagine not, because it would not be of the heart. The Almighty wants you to freely give Him control over your life. All He wants is to show you a better way to live, so that you can be happy. I'm not going to say that it is going to be easy, but you must first be willing. Building a true relationship with The Holy Spirit cannot be done, until you invite Him in. He is not one that will force His way in, but He will show you who He is. *Luke 6:47 – 49 "Whosoever cometh to me, and heareth my sayings, and doeth them, I will shew you to whom he is like:"* The Almighty wants to show Himself to you, but He cannot avail Himself to anyone. That is the same manner of respect that we need to present ourselves with. You must guard your heart and protect

I can't take one more thing!

the Anointing inside. Many do not have enough self-respect and that is why their lives are full of assailants. Only, because they let them in!

Mothers protect their young, but grandparents go beyond the seed of a mother's womb and their protection doubles. Grandparents are normally more sensitive with the needs of their grandchildren and they tend to spoil them with love. They will do far more than parents, just to protect their grandchildren. Of course, they know that their young could not survive without them. They love going that extra mile. So they are prepared to feed them, clothe them, carry them and so forth. Grandchildren get so much more respect from grandparents than their own parents. However, grandparents are more knowledgeable than parents, because they have already traveled the road of motherhood or fatherhood. When you love someone, you will do all that is necessary to protect them. In addition, if we are created in God's image then surely we need to protect what's inside of us! Always be very considerate of how others treat you and respect you. If people beat you down, then they are tearing the best

I can't take one more thing!

out of you. It is hard trying to live a good life if one is surrounded by people that have no heart for them. Truly, it is harder when you are sleeping with your own enemy. The ones that are close to you are normally the ones that assault you more. It is a shame how the ones you love and spend a lifetime with assault you more. It is awful. Many have allowed it to go on so long, until they become prone to unthoughtful love. Although, that is not love at all. When someone loves you, they will spend more time to help bring the best out of you. It may not always be perfect, but they will always respect you. Love simply respects. Protect all that is inside by being willing to allow Jesus to be your Almighty!

Isaiah 54:17 "No weapon that is formed against thee shall prosper; and every tongue that shall rise against thee in judgment thou shall condemn. This is the heritage of the servants of the Lord, and their righteousness is of me, saith the Lord." The more of God you have in you, the less victory your weapon will have to destroy you. People of The Almighty need to allow The Spirit of Jesus to rise up within them. It is

I can't take one more thing!

a privilege that GOD can use us in any form or fashion to do His work. It does not matter what your duty is or vision. It is The Most High in yourselves that is going to accomplish the work. So therefore, let no weapon formed against you be prosperous. *Isaiah 54:17 "No weapon that is formed against thee shall prosper; and every tongue that shall rise against thee in judgment thou shall condemn.* This is the heritage of the servants of the Lord, and their righteousness is of me, saith the Lord."

This scripture is the key to life and that is the reason I continue to use it so much. God intends for all of His servants to inherit this RIGHT! He does not want any weapon, enemy, person or thing to destroy His servants. We should not allow things or people to destroy what God is doing in us and purposed for us. Our mind should be on The Most High in that manner, because He is more powerful than any weapon. There is none that can destroy Him! Nothing should be able to stop, hinder or hurt you as long as you believe in Him.

I can't take one more thing!

Time after time many forget what caused them to believe. Always pray for others. You will be amazed how others' living conditions are purposed for you to see. That is another way to see what kind of heart you have. It is not for you to judge, but see if you have the right heart intent. Surely, it is good to look upon your life and notice change. When one starts noticing others in prayer, then a change of heart is taking place. Most definitely, this particular Pharisee was giving God praise for his personal accomplishments. *Luke 18:11 "The Pharisee stood and thus with himself, God I thank thee, that I am not as other men are, extortionists, unjust, adulterers, or even as this publican."* He was praying for self and forgot to lift up the publican in prayer. However, the publican came to God as a sinner and asked for mercy. He acknowledged God in all his faults, and asked God to be merciful unto him. He also humbled himself in a manner being poor in the spirit, and needing to be improved. He took absolutely no credit for righteousness as the Pharisee, but giving all credit to God. Notice, when you come being poor in spirit, The

I can't take one more thing!

Almighty will fill you with mercy. Make sure you also pray for others as you pray. It may be the only prayer they receive that day. Another way to destroy your enemies, is to pray for them.

Luke 18:12 "I fast twice a week and I give tithes of all that I possess." The Pharisee was lifting up what he does for God instead of what God has done for him. However, the publican needed God and wanted Him with a true heart. He was depending on The Almighty to supply Him. In addition, the publican humbled himself. He realized that he could do nothing without God and immediately he was justified through the mercies of God. Whenever God can come in and justify you, He will be your supreme defender. He will begin working within you to fortify His Spirit through you, and that will begin to spread power flowing out of your belly and heart to strengthen you. That will remove any substantial buildup of doubt, fear, incompleteness, weakness, and strongholds. He wants you purged through His WORD! He will stand in your favor, and align you up within His will. *Matthew 12:34 "O generation of vipers, how can ye, being evil,*

I can't take one more thing!

speak good things? for out of the abundance of the heart the mouth speaketh." He does not need anyone to talk about how good He is, but show someone His power. The way He thinks is powerful. He did not have to labor, when He created this earth. He just spoke it into existence and it was so. At times in our lives, we tend to put more thought on our personal situation than on the power of God. Just because sometimes things look to be cloudy, we walk around as if we are walking in fog and cannot see. Have you ever been in a foggy situation and could not see your way out? Your time is right now; the fog in your life must disappear especially when you speak with power. At all times, you must allow GOD to lead you into a faith that makes all things possible. Learn how to speak with authority. Do not be afraid, for fearing the enemy in your life will destroy you. However, speaking with authority will make your enemy afraid and then he will flee away from you.

Luke 18:13 "And the publican, standing afar off, would not lift up so much as his eyes unto heaven, but smote upon his breast, saying, God be merciful to me

I can't take one more thing!

a sinner." At all times, we must allow GOD to be GOD over every weapon that arises against us. If God spoke life into creation on this earth and then formed man afterwards, know that He can change your situation within a blink of an eye? When He created light He said, "Let there be light", and it was. Just like your life, GOD is waiting for you to confess and be honest. He wants HIS WORD to speak life into you and for you to speak life with His WORD. He wants to change and deliver your life from sin. The purer you are, the more power God will give you. He created this world just by speaking to something that was void. He brought forth so much beauty and life along with it. Do you think that GOD is going to let anything come up against His people and destroy them? Absolutely not! Job's life story is one of the finest examples in history. *Job 23:10 "But he knoweth the way I take: when he hath tried me, I shall come forth as gold."* God already knows our coming out as we are tried. Trials, tribulations, life assaults, aggravations, persecutions and more are ways we are tried. Job understood what and why He was going through.

I can't take one more thing!

Though at times he also complained and grew bitter, he held on. No trying time will be easy. Many are in a lot of pain, so much until many cannot endure. *Job 5:2 "O that my grief were thoroughly weighed, and my calamity laid in the balances."* At times you must see your life for what it is and still trust The Most High. When hurtful things try to destroy your faith, you still must still trust Him. Growing pains are not easy to endure, but we must because victory is in our trust. If you trust your situation over The Almighty, then your situation is your God and it will ruin you.

A few years ago, GOD gave me a sermon for every action there is a reaction. Every test that we endure and with every action we show others how GOD is in us. He is going to allow us to reap just what we have sowed. The weapons purposed to destroy you are only going to multiply your faith. We must seek God in a childlike form, expecting Him to be our Father. The publican sought God as an infant's faith. Infants depend solely on others, they can do nothing for themselves. He did not allow His sin to stop him from calling on God, and neither was he exalting himself.

I can't take one more thing!

He prayed for God to have mercy on him and He did. *Ephesians 3:16 "That he would grant you, according to the riches of His glory, to be strengthened with might by his Spirit in the inner man."* A true believer in the word of The Almighty is going to stand no matter how hard the wind blows.

Even Job feared as his flesh rose. His faith was unsteady. There are times when we are tried that our flesh will cause fear to keep us in a going through state. *Job 21:6 "Even when I remember I am afraid, and trembling taketh hold on my flesh."* Trying times are seasonal, but your faith is going to calculate your season. As soon as one matures in faith, and believes, the sooner one can be delivered. Faith must age as one is being spiritually developed, that is how WISDOM is birthed! How you are drawn up may not be required of me. It depends on who you are purposed to become. I knew my goal was great. So therefore, the trials that I endured were to balance my faith. The Most High wants us evenly weighed and our faith unsteady!

I can't take one more thing!

When I was a Co-Pastor, I thought my faith was great. At times, when we appear to be strong in one area, we are needing to be strengthened in another. Yes, it was all it needed to be for that moment in my life. Literally, it was greater than it previously was. There were a lot of things I thought I was sound in. Nevertheless, as I lived a little while longer, I begin to experience life in an unusual way. Figured I was going to lose my mind. Be careful what and how you pray, because in many cases our trials are just our answered prayers. I will never forget, my uncle said, "She must have prayed for a lot!" He was looking at my storms. He saw how I was being greatly assaulted from every angle of my life. The enemy had no mercy on me and, he assaulted me with all and all. While others were looking in, I was just trying to survive. Every weapon was trying to destroy my faith in The Most High. In addition, The Most High was introducing me to become a FAITH WARRIOR! He was teaching me how to war. I had previously conquered other tests and, I know I pleased Him. However, now He began the big test and, I came through those as well. None

I can't take one more thing!

were easy! When you are being tried, accept it with gladness and praise. If you have prayed for a lot and it is not coming forth, then once you defeat this attack from the enemy you will be closer to your answered prayers. Job knew it personally well. As you are being tried, you may not always appear pretty in the eyesight of man, but as long as you do not give up on your faith, you will be all right. Whatever your trial, let it make you appear to be a better you and get your gold out of it as Job did. Make sure you get double for your trouble!

Job 21:6, "Even when I remember I am afraid, and trembling taketh hold on my flesh." When the strongholds of your life are stronger than you, then you need the immediate strength you have never known. You need the strength of a Shield to protect you from the fiery darts of life. You need a mountain Rock, to cover you when the forces of the enemy are roaring against you and the Oil of your Butter to give you sliding ability; a King that can give you perfect direction, lead you out of the pattern of destruction; also, a Shepherd to look after you when you are

I can't take one more thing!

headed in harm's way. He is a Judge that will correct you when you are inconceivably wrong; a Refuge that will fight your battle during the times you give up. He has a Fortress of power that you can gain victorious strength of the highest capacity. He is an Avenger to avenge your death in the case of a wounded heart and, He has the power to demolish any weapon that has formed against you. Our Heavenly Father is a Creator that can speak anything into existence. He is someone that has the availability that will surely deliver you out of any situation because you believed without a shadow of a doubt against the enemy of confusion. He is a Miraculous Healer when the doctors tell you there is nothing that they can do, because He is the Savior of all the earth. He's a Protector from all hurt, harm, danger, and evil. He is a Provider of sufficiency, so that every need in your life will be bountifully met and met on time; and a Redeemer to awaken any dead thing within you, so that your soul will be granted the Eternal Life promised with pure happiness and peace. He is my Prince of Peace. He is Mercy forever more and full of Grace. In addition, Jesus is the truth,

I can't take one more thing!

always showing me the way towards His marvelous Light.

I can't take one more thing!

Aggravated Assault On Your Mind

"God's WORD is your Defense!"
~Parice C. Parker

I can't take one more thing!

Aggravated Assault On Your Mind

CHAPTER 11
God's Word Is Your Defense

> *"In your days of trouble, The WORD shall fight your battle!"*
> ~ *Parice C. Parker*

I can't take one more thing!

CHAPTER 11

God's Word Is Your Defense

It is time to depend on The Most High, like never before. Believe and stand as a solider girded up with the truth. Prepared to fight and win. Perhaps, many spiritually die as they are being tried. Probably because they have not been properly trained to war! They did not take the time to equip themselves in the Word and with The Holy Spirit! *11 Samuel 22:35 He teacheth my hands to war; so that a bow of steel is broken by mine arms.* I know there are many word inclined people, but few are spiritual! Actually, they can quote scriptures that many preachers cannot. They know them inside out, but literally have not spent quality time getting personal with The Spirit of Jesus. Anyone can memorize a scripture, but not many can

I can't take one more thing!

get acquainted with Jesus. When one notices the power of The WORD that is when life comes forth. Life is in the WORD, not a quote! *John 1:1 In the beginning was the WORD, and the WORD was with God, and the WORD was God.* Jesus was in the beginning and He is The WORD. Many that delete Jesus out of their life, also, remove the WORD. The WORD works through Jesus and He is the Light of the WORD! Figuratively, they are inseparable. Want life, get Jesus! Even a void place know the power that is within the WORD. *Genesis 1:1&2,* this earth was without form and it was void, but when the WORD entered and The SPIRIT of I AM moved, it was developed. Once the WORD was spoken, then it begin to move. Your life will grow to its fullness when you speak the WORD. A quote is only repeating what someone says. Almost to the exact and some paraphrase because it has been documenting in many ways. However, living in the WORD grants new life at all times. It causes one to triumph in victory, and not misery! Especially, when one is confident in Jesus. How, can one be sure if they do not believe? The

I can't take one more thing!

WORD will back you up. All you have to do is look at one's life and the WORD should be speaking. *John 10:10, the enemies only purpose is to kill, steal, and destroy The Truth out of you. Notice when one get a hold of The Truth (JESUS) prosperity is evident.* No, it is not a money thing. Prosperity is The WORD, presenting itself in abundance. Notice if you cannot see immediate substance, you can see their vision. Jesus comes that we might have live and life more abundantly. He never purposed for us to live in lack. That is not how He function. Actually, lack is the opposite of abundance! When one recognizes who Jesus is, then power is revealed in their lives. How can He obtain glory out of slackness and laziness? Where there is no production, then there is no life. Jesus is life in the WORD. *John 4:23 He waits on his believers to worship Him in Spirit and in truth!* Once one understands the Truth they are freed from bondage! That is why it is valuable to believe in Jesus, because once you know Him He will fit Himself in you with The WORD. The WORD only works when, it enters. No matter how much one quote or

I can't take one more thing!

paraphrase. If one do not receive the WORD in their ear, then one will not see results. Once The WORD enters your heart, it will begin to show you things that are prepared for your future if you endure. An example, if someone attacked you and they threaten your life what would you do? The only thing will be in your mind is survival. Perhaps, you have a love one that you want to see, again. So therefore, you fight to stay alive. During assaults we all must have a strategy to fight and win. If not we might die. However, the picture that is in your mind is what is keeping you alive and giving you a drive to fight your assailant. In the same manner, that is how The WORD needs to enter in our hearts and show us a spiritual portfolio of what's to come as we endure. It must enter in, and Jesus goes nowhere that He is not welcomed! *1 Corinthians 2:9, "But as it is written, EYE HATH NOT SEEN, NOR EAR HEARD, NEITHER HAVE ENTERED INTO THE HEART OF MAN, THE THINGS WHICH GOD HATH PREPARED FOR THEM THAT LOVE HIM."* God prepares the ones He loves with the best that life offers. Most people, do not

I can't take one more thing!

realize how much He has in store for them, because they cannot see with their spiritual eyes. If one cannot see spiritually, then one is spiritual blind. They simply, do not know Him spiritually. Aggravations only intent is to destroy, kill or steal something from you. Find its purpose and then you will understand what the enemy wants from you. Satan seeks to find ways to destroy you, and aim to find a way to rid Jesus out of your life. He will come with the most outrageous things to cause conflict within your faith. Want all that God has prepared for you, then cause Him to move on your life and get fit in JESUS! Once you mate with Him, He is yours and you are His. You will be a match, made in heaven.

One cannot live in curses and blesses at once. Your life will speak for one or the other. *Galatians 3:10, "For as many as are for the works of the law are under the curse: for it is written, CURSED IS EVERY ONE THAT CONTINUETH NOT IN ALL THIINGS WHICH ARE WRITTEN IN THE BOOK OF THE LAW TO DO THEM."* Remember on the mountain when Satan tried to tempt Jesus, he couldn't. Jesus was

I can't take one more thing!

too spiritual for Satan. Satan might know the scriptures, but he could not know Jesus. For years he has been trying to figure Him out and couldn't. Jesus simply would not be friend His enemy. Many get acquainted with the enemy of Jesus, just to have a friend. If someone dis liked my God, I would not want to be their friend. If Jesus is The Most High in your life, then why please His enemy? That is a No, No! A lot of people befriend the enemies of Jesus and then expects Him to save them. On the other hand, they refuse the rewards being obedience guarantees and exchange it for the destruction disobedience causes. In addition, if Jesus had to pray forty days and nights after coming into contact with Satan, then what makes you think that you do not? He is all spiritual! Many take Satan for granted, and still continue in sin. A one night prayer is just the beginning of your deliverance, but one must continue at least 39 more days of loyalty to Jesus. Maybe by then, one will be able to stand more righteous! That is how powerful the contact of Satan is, and many play with him every day of their lives. Jesus knew what to do and He was fuel up with

I can't take one more thing!

heavenly power. It took Him 40 days of persistent and continuance in prayer, to be completely fuel up! Pray, consistently! Nevertheless, Satan is your assailant and he hates you! Never think that you are too strong for him to enter, just stay away! He is not your friend! Note, Jesus is all powerful and He prayed diligently. We all must do the same, especially after coming into contact with the enemy.

Satan also thought he had Job figured out, boy was he surprised. Do not let him figure you, disfigure him. Aggravation is purposed to destroy, do not let it enter. Satan wants to disfigure the image of Jesus in you. So, that he can discredit His WORD. Without WORD, there is no life and without life no abundance. That is why it is so much confliction when one calls upon Jesus, than any other name. This name possess powers and reveals truth. *John 8:32 The Truth shall make you free. The enemy does not want you to know the truth that is why he is always popping up with assaults.* However, one that truly know Jesus must be shaped spiritually. Satan is no match for the remade in Jesus! Ones relationship with Jesus will be too close and

I can't take one more thing!

Satan will not be able to fit the question in their mind. If, Jesus exist? Their life will be a living testimony! All they would have to do, is look back over their life and know that He is The Almighty. Your testimony will prove that you are a for sure witness, because of facts that the WORD is proof for your life. DO NOT ENTERTAIN AND BE IN THE SAME COMPANY AS NON BELIVERS IN JESUS. THEY MIGHT TRY TO CONVERT YOU. IT COULD CAUSE YOUR SOUL TO SPEND ENTERNITY WHERE JESUS HAVE NO PURPOSE! When you apply for a job, most applications have a part for you to note your experience. It does not add up to listen to someone that has absolutely no experience in Jesus. Once one truly know Jesus, there should have been a match made in heaven. I know He is my Heavenly mate and no god could take His place. I would not let one that has no experience in serving Jesus to convince me, in converting my faith. That is the number one reason Satan has so many under his command, because of faith converters. Never let no one introduce their god to you! It should not even fit into your spirit. I cannot

I can't take one more thing!

imagine sitting around listening to others considering my mom unfit and not real. I would not let people destroy my belief in my mother. Why let them destroy your belief in Jesus? The enemy is purposed to only cause destruction in your faith! If one is against Jesus, they are against you too! In John 10:10 it explains the purpose of Jesus, so that many will have life in abundance. His WORD is your defenses magnesium. Do not look for all the scriptures in the bible to explain poorness, but look up the ones that guarantees blessing and favor from The Most High. Proverbs 8:11 Getting WISDOM will cause you to inherit substance and He will fill your treasures. Now, look at your life, what is it adding you up to be. You calculate it? Is it what the WORD say? Some things are just common sense, and that is something everyone does not have.

Only one has the power to teach you, and He is I AM! *(Exodus 3:13-14)* You must know your commander. There is power to revealed through The WORD and it will be your defense. But, you must know The WORD and how to utilize it! *PSALMS 86:7, "IN THE DAY OF MY TROUBLE, I WILL*

I can't take one more thing!

CALL UPON THEE: FOR THOU WILT ANSWER ME." When trouble comes, that could be a dangerous thing because harm is there to destroy your mind. However, God is there to make you indestructible.

Stress will try to move in and embark your mind causing delusional effects within your faith. Worrying about your aggravations will anger you and it can cause you, to take your mind off GOD. Imputing either fear within your spirit that you may not make it or either girded in the truth ready to overcome. Trouble can only cause a mind effect, so let it not trouble you because God has your back. Bishop L. D. Parker once preached this message," The Devil is Up Set because He Has Peeped Into Your Future." If you are not going to be a threat to the enemy, he has no need to assault you. Why make an effort to assault a mind already wasted? You are called to duty to operate in the army of The Most High. Yes, He expects you to be unbeatable! Significant change is getting ready to take place in your life. Moreover, the enemy knows all about it. That is why you are now a target. You are a threat to the enemy and He is mad at

I can't take one more thing!

you. The Devil main tactic is to assault your mind, make you think you cannot win this thing because He wants you to throw in your towel. He wants to slow you down and cause you to sink into your situation. Look down, you are not in quicksand so move forward. Do not let the enemy destroy your life. You have the right now power to change! God has given you weapons of every sort, but you must know how to use them. Hold your ground, stand on His WORD. *Galatians 6:7 "Be not deceived; God is not mocked: for whatsoever a man soweth, that shall he also reap."*

A solider only enlists themselves into a service agreement to serve and to fight. Their cause is to serve and protect their country. If you are not prepared, then you will lose. If you have no purpose, then you are already defeated. The sole purpose for a solider is to fight the battle, until he wins. A solider signs up prepared for war. They learn their weapons and its purpose. A solider will be able to defend others in case of an emergency, because their trained to fight more than one at a time. They are trained to war and to

I can't take one more thing!

execute their assailants! What's senseless to others, is valuable to a solider. Get to know your weapons and how to use them. Every weapon has a purpose, just as every enemy that comes after you. Once a solider is trained, they understand patience. They are trained to wait, with an expectancy to fight for life and their purpose is to defeat their enemy! Do not think you can fight alone, that is why the WORD of GOD teaches us to forsake not the assembly of the saints. During the time of our assembling, (coming together in agreement) the instructions are given on how to battle. Teaching us how to operate, come out victorious and strengthening us through knowledge. You must study and know your weapon, while you are getting prepared for the attack. The reason why soldiers are so confident, is because they are not alone. Other soldiers are trained to look after one another. *Galatians 6:6"Let him that is taught in the word communicate unto him that teacheth in all good things."*

Isaiah 65 (24) "And it shall come to pass, that before they call, I will answer; and while they are yet speaking, I will hear." He already know your need

I can't take one more thing!

before you pray! Although sometimes we feel that GOD has turned a deaf ear, well He has not. He is just consuming the wrongness within our lives and readjusting our faith. He did not create you to leave you. Take time out and talk to GOD, He shall renew your strength. Once again, I can assure you The Almighty has looked at your situation and know your outcome is going to be awesome. God knows our hearts that is how we are affected by the power of GOD. He changes and corrects our hearts by moving with power through our situations. He is also waiting for us to depend on HIM. *Galatians 6:9 "And let us not be weary in well doing: for in due season we shall reap, if we faint not.* You are not alone and you are going to come through this thing, but you must endure! Trust in the power of GOD through the blood of JESUS, that it is over and done. Know that your season is here. GOD has given you power in the name of JESUS, and as long as you have JESUS you have all you need. There is going to always be some form of assault tactic to try you. It is up to the power that lives within you, to introduce hell to your I AM. It is

I can't take one more thing!

your choice to exalt The Almighty in you. *Galatians 6:9 "And let us not be weary in well doing: for in due season we shall reap, if we faint not."*

Without the fear of GOD in your heart in a good way then you have no power. Fearing Him is reverencing Him. Through the fear of GOD, you gain the opportunity to be powerful in His WORD? Without power, the enemy will defeat you. The enemy is not afraid of the fearless, but the ones that reverence the WORD. Also, he cannot have anything that we do not give him nor can he take anything that we do not hand over. *Ephesians 6:1 "For we wrestle not against flesh and blood, but against principalities, against powers, against the rulers of the darkness of this world, against spiritual wickedness in high places."*

The enemy will try all day long to destroy you and he will attack you with any weapon that he forms against you, if you do not belong to God; when you believe in The Most High, then you are covered by the power of Jesus. Regardless of what you are going

I can't take one more thing!

through, whether it is your health deteriorating, your marriage failing, your household is crumbling, your child wandering, your job situation or even if you don't have two pennies to rub together, this assault is not yours to fight. I believe that GOD is just magnifying His power in you. The God we serve does not walk out and leave us during our most aggravated moments. However, He does work greater in us through the aggravation, in order to make us become who He is preparing us to be. He wants us to know Him in a manner that we once thought was unreal. *Ephesians 6:13 "Wherefore take unto you the whole Armor of God, that ye may be able to withstand in the evil day, and having done all, to stand."* If you do not know when you are being attacked, you will be in serious trouble. Realistically, the time is now to never leave home without your proper Armor.

Job 21:6, "Even when I remember I am afraid, and trembling taketh hold on my flesh." When the strongholds of your life are stronger than you, then you need the immediate strength you have never known. You need the strength of a Shield to protect

I can't take one more thing!

you from the fiery darts of life. You need a mountain Rock, to cover you when the forces of the enemy are roaring against you and the Oil of your Butter to give you sliding ability. A King that can give you perfect direction, lead you out of the pattern of destruction; also, a Shepherd to look after you when you are headed in harm's way. He is a Judge that will correct you when you are inconceivably wrong; a Refuge that will fight your battle during the times you give up. He has a Fortress of power that you can gain victorious strength of the highest capacity. He is an Avenger to avenge your death in the case of a wounded heart and He has the power to demolish any weapon that has formed against you. Our Heavenly Father is a Creator that can speak anything into existence. He is someone that has the availability that will surely deliver you out of any situation because you believed without a shadow of a doubt against the enemy of confusion. He is a Miraculous Healer when the doctors tell you there is nothing that they can do, because He is the Savior of all the earth. He's a Protector from all hurt, harm, danger, and evil. He is a Provider of sufficiency, so

I can't take one more thing!

that every need in your life will be bountifully met and met on time; and a Redeemer to awaken any dead thing within you, so that your soul will be granted the Eternal Life promised with pure happiness and peace. He is my Prince of Peace. He is Mercy forever more and full of Grace. In addition, Jesus is the truth, always showing me the way towards His marvelous Light.

I can't take one more thing!

Aggravated Assault On Your Mind

> *"Becoming a Champion Is Never Easy!"*
> *~Parice C. Parker*

I can't take one more thing!

Aggravated Assault On Your Mind

CHAPTER 12
Skin For Skin

> *"What Price Are You Willing To Pay To Prove Your Loyalty To The Most High?"*
> *~ Parice C. Parker*

I can't take one more thing!

CHAPTER 12

Skin For Skin

When one stands, they do not have time to sit. Their tears will no longer fall on their face because they're all cried out! Just when you think GOD is bringing you out of one transition, then here comes another trying to destroy your victory. The enemy works on each one of us in a different manner. If the enemy can stop your progression, then he can stop your fate. That is why the enemy is trying his best to immobilize you, so you will not go forth. If he wins, then one cannot progress. However, if you continue believing in the power of Jesus. Many others will be inspired by seeing your victory. GOD knows your outcome, but do you? He wants you to see what He sees in you. Now, faith is so important, and you will

I can't take one more thing!

need it to survive to achieve. Run on, so you can overcome. What a joyous day that will be? At this point in your life, GOD is ordering your steps. *Ephesians 6:15 "And your feet shod with the preparation of the gospel of peace;"* GOD cannot mend something that is not broken, and He cannot fix something that is already repaired. Do not worry, your steps are already ordered, but it is in His word. Through your faith, you shall be made whole. That is why you need to stay consistent in the WORD; it will increase you in your time of need and help you to endure. It will also boost your faith and keep you charged up and ready to go! Faith without works is dead. GOD does not need another quitter on His team. *Ephesians 6:14 "Stand, therefore, having our loins girt about with truth, and having on the breastplate of righteousness."* He needs an elite soldier that is fully prepared to fight and be unbeatable. He wants a boxer to step into the ring, and the first punch to knockout. Certainly, He needs a trained marathon runner prepared to run the necessary miles to reach their goal and be a winner. No weapon that is formed against

I can't take one more thing!

you shall prosper, because GOD has the power to destroy any man-made weapon. No one can interrupt, stop nor override the power of The Most High in you. Once you become a Jesus believer and excel in faith, you will soon be able to put up a do not disturb sign for the enemy! He will no longer bother you. There is a reliable protection you must show forth that covers you, and it must be potent! Once Job received double for his trouble, there is no other time that the enemy tried him again. *Ephesians 6:16 "Above all, taking the shield of faith, wherewith ye shall be able to quench all the fiery darts of the wicked."* Though torment comes in life, continue to give up the wrong for the right. Make sure you are well dressed and girded up for battle and show the enemy your faith! Stand and fight, become unbeatable! Our faith in Jesus will cover us from the fire of our trials, just like Job. Going through a great trial will cause you not only to war but give you advance techniques to win. The way you fight must be improved. Every trial is purposed to test your war ability in different ways. Do not take it personally, God loves you, but He is showing the

I can't take one more thing!

enemy that you love Him too. *Job 1:10 & 11, Satan wanted to prove to The Most High that he could cause Job to curse his faith!* Just think of the worst trial you have had to endure. Surely, you made it out once, and you will make it through this. Although, many do not realize how they curse Jesus and die. Every time one turns their back on Jesus as they are being tried, they begin to be a living example of a Jesus murderer. I can imagine that is how Job felt, as he held on to his faith. He did not want to be the cause of the death of The Almighty. So, therefore, he held on to his faith and showed others the value of faith. I know things grew terrible for him, but he could not accept that God had turned His back on his needs! Yes, trials will break you down, but they will also cause you to stand more righteous. I do not stand the way I used to hold. Now my posture is straighter. I stand as though I'm on guard. After you go through so much, you will not carry yourself in the same manner. Your faith will be more alert, and you will always be prepared to battle. You will no longer be a loser, but a champion of war!

I can't take one more thing!

A champion will always be determined to win! My purpose was fulfilled every time I went to church. I went to be informed of the WORD; I needed to survive, and I received! I realized that the WORD and I had a lot in common. We both loved to fight, and we both love to win. We had one more thing in common, we did not accept being a failure, and we felt that all things were possible! As I continue to grow in the WORD, then the WORD begins to develop mine purposefully in me. It helps me grow strong and taught me many different techniques on how to overcome. I am not talking about hypocrisy. I am talking about being true through the word of GOD and receiving every new WORD unto my ear and letting it adapt to my heart. Therefore, my footsteps are ordered by the Lord. Also, every Wednesday night I attended Bible study faithfully and tremendously began to grow in the WORD of The Most High. I considered the WORD to be right; being fully committed to presenting myself worthy of praise. I just begin to LOVE the WORD! Do not let a day go without studying. You must prepare yourself faithfully to sustain. Meditation is

I can't take one more thing!

needed daily, and singing a good inspirational song will always keep you inspired! Kneeling daily and reverencing The Almighty; just making a drastic change for the better will cause you to want to get even closer to His presence. However, you must make The WORD personal in your life and spend quality time mating with The WORD! Get Intimate and let The WORD enter! See, before all this ever took place I was a terrible gambler, a drinker of alcohol and living the clubbing lifestyle. I occasionally used profanity and was a major gossiper. However, one day I was dying for a change. After I had just been on a winning streak at the casino; still there was no joy. I got aggravated with myself, and I began feeling the irritation. I needed something greater than myself. Business was great, I had money, and things were going well in my life. I still was not happy. Just a reminder, we all have blemishes within our lives. Do not let a blemish or a weapon stay formed against you. *Ephesians 6:17 "And take the helmet of salvation, and the sword of the Spirit, which is the word of God."* The Most High can go wherever you can, and if you

I can't take one more thing!

need Him, He will be there. Everywhere you go, take Him with you and if you can't, do not go! Believing in Him is freedom from every stronghold in our life. Nothing can tie Him down, chain Him up and that is the same power we can have in The Most High every day. God is power, and you can have as much of Him as you desire. Though things have tried me I still had to ask myself, is it worth it? When I wanted to turn back, I could not. When I wanted to give up, I would not. God will always keep you in remembrance of Him, just to keep your faith focused. Pressures in your life will weigh you down, but God will be right there to pick you up. At about 1:30 am I wanted to give up and run out in my life. I heard a voice. It said to me again more boldly than ever. "Just write your anger on paper, you can't go wrong that way!" So, I began to write this.

(My First Writings- My First Known Gift)

There are times of trouble, heartaches, headaches, distress and long-suffering. There are trials of much unbearable pain, feeling defeated,

I can't take one more thing!

decomposition, dissatisfaction, nowhere to turn and nowhere to hide! Every shoulder that has come by, but still, no shoulder to lean on. No help, and others no remorse. Only, regretful letdowns! I need, and I have longed for a friend. A friend of understanding, trust worthy, loving, and most of all sincere. Someone just to hold when I'm lonely, and catch me when I'm falling. Someone I actually can depend on, and share my most inner feelings. Most of all sincere. A loving friend, not ever being selfish or unforgiving. A friend that I can reconcile my differences. A friend will never leave me nor forsake me. A friend to forgive me when I do wrong. Understand I am not perfect, and I realize that I am only human. I know that I am going to make a mistake here or there. It comforts me to know that I have a friend who cares.

I need a friend that does not hold a grudge or envy me. Also, a friend that sincerely accepts my apologies and forgives me when I apologize. I am seeking a friend loaded with pure compassion and a tender loving heart. When I cry, my friend cries and can relocate my situation and help wipe the tears

I can't take one more thing!

away. I have lived my life playing Russian roulette; however, not intentionally, but unintentionally. My friend one day had mercy upon my soul, reached down for me by offering a helping hand and I grasped on. Now, I refuse to let go. I was of flesh, but I realized my heart was full of compassion. Yes, I was willing to die for a change. Daily I thank GOD for my friend because he had mercy upon my soul.

One dark, pitch black night with a beloved moon, glowing upon the stars in the midnight sky, out of the darkness, there I saw a glimmering light. I recognized spontaneously through my darkest hours that there is still a glowing light. The moon was my inspiration. All my life I have lived among supposed to be friends, with absolutely no intention of surpassing a heart-filled sincere love. It was only like to generate a benefit. I guess they could gain something of me. So I kneeled down realizing I had nothing, but a void in my life! No meaning, no love, no one could supply the need I have personally longed. Loneliness was my best friend. My heart began to throb with a passionate intellect, only being

I can't take one more thing!

energized and flamed by the Spirit of Jesus. In my living room, my heart began to churn for fullness, and I started to pour out the meaningless filth that hindered me from my friend.

Asking in the name of JESUS for forgiveness realizing I had been of no goodness to Him. However, He has always been there and always good to me. I prayed without ceasing and giving no opening for the enemy to complicate my desire to be fulfilled. I wanted a definite change, being spiritually motivated, no longer feeling meaningless, and only being supplied with fullness. The Holy Spirit began to move all about me. Desirable fullness, flaming like fire embedded all in me. Praying without ceasing and knowing not what to pray, but that I ought to pray. Seeking and yes, so wonderfully received the power of the Holy Spirit, through the blood of my friend. When I talk to my friend, I attain a highly accelerating uplifter. An inspirational thrive, deep- embedded within my heart, soul body and mind. No flesh shall overthrow, no devil from hell to devour victorious victory, no tests of trials of tribulation shall cause a

I can't take one more thing!

mince of a doubt of the sincerity of this friend. No defeat from the enemy, no mind of the human flesh shall be a corrupt heart, of the love of this friend. Together we stand, surely divided I will fall. A friend indeed. Oh, what a friend I have found in JESUS.

Ephesians 6:18 "Praying always with all prayer and supplication in the Spirit, and watching thereunto with all perseverance and supplication for all saints." Hold onto your faith and walk with The ALMIGHTY. Just as he delivered Job, He will also deliver you. The weapons in your life might tend to slow you down, but it is for your good. You may think the world is against you. Still, GOD is allowing you to be strengthened so that no man or enemy on this earth and beneath could ever stop you or, perhaps, cause you to be stopped! You may also think that the pressures of your life are over boiling, but GOD is releasing some strongholds out of you. You may think GOD has forsaken you, but He is creating His power within you. The night I begin to write, I was angry at the world and frustrated with my life. I felt every aggravation. My life aggravations were intended to

I can't take one more thing!

assault my mind until it afflicted my soul. I yearned in prayer as I wrote my feelings down on a piece of paper. I felt the miseries that life had offered me. If I had never felt my life aggravations, I would have never become who God wanted me to be. A Life of Prosperity was birthed out of my aggravation, as I was being afflicted. Unlimited increases occurred out of my assaults. My mind was made up to stand and wait on the Lord. I knew then I was chosen, because at this point late in the midnight hour, God created in me a way out. Ever since then, I have been writing my way out and using the gifts God has given me to cause my mind not to feel the pressures of life. God is my life defender, and as long as I know He is in control, no weapon has the power to harm me. I speak with the power of Jesus that blesses will overtake you as you endure. You must speak the Word into entire existence so that God can operate it in your life. Knowing who He is in your life will cause your steps to be covered. As long as you know God is on your side, no rock or hard place will stop you. There may be many attacks on your life trying to disable your power, but God will

I can't take one more thing!

deliver you. Hold on to God's Word, let His Word be a powerful mark in your life. Astonish others with your faith!

Under no circumstances can anyone or anything ever retain you against your will, unless you are taken by surprise or caught off guard. Surely, the assailant of destruction may introduce the weapon to you, but the assailant is restrained from all its power to demolish you. The Most High will be your Divine Protector from every evil force. No matter the probability of the weapon that is formed, as long as you allow GOD to be your daily covering that weapon cannot cause you harm. Quite naturally, the WORD states that the Lord will not put more on you than you can bear. If GOD knew that He could not bring you out, He would not have allowed you to go through. GOD always has a designated plan for all His children and He will do whatever it takes to make you recognize, who's the head. *Ephesians 6:20 "For which I am an ambassador in bonds: that therein I may speak boldly as I ought to speak."* When one is angry, they may say anything, and words are

I can't take one more thing!

powerful! Many just talk too much. Too much talk and not enough action. When one is angry, they may talk a good game and no change. However, when one has had enough, then it's show time. I let life beat me up so bad, I almost died. At my next breath, I began to fight. I realized my life only represented my belief and my talk. I spoke a good game, but through my life assaults, I had to prove that His WORD is all powerful. My courage was no match for my talk. However, my talk had to encourage my walk. The more I begin to speak The WORD, the more my life began to manifest in His favor! *Ephesians 6:24 "Grace be with all them that love our Lord Jesus Christ in sincerity." Amen*

Know who you are in the Lord, know your heart is sincere, and He is your Maker. Once you realize the depth of your love for Him, then you will know that His grace covers you. When grace covers you, mercy is always present. As I experienced many terrible things in my life, I held on to God. Though we get angry at times, we must hang on and allow our anger to be overturned to become our power! Find the

I can't take one more thing!

one real possibility that could come out of aggravation and hold on to it! God has the power to make things right and sometimes He will allow things to appear wrong before we appear right! Every life assault aggravated me and caused me grief! Afterward, I desired to understand Him more. The same happened to Jonah. Though he grew faint, it made him cry out to God. After we finish running away from our calling, then we will move to our duty and stand! We all have a moment that will make us become obedient or face death. Also, when that moment comes nothing can change your mind from that point on. Know who you are and whose you are. I know I am a child of The Most High and He only produces righteousness. It does not matter what others think of me, or how people treat me as long as I know The Almighty loves me. His love is enough for me to become more than a conqueror! Love The Most High greater and watch Him work in your life. He will work some things out of you, that you never knew existed. He did it for me, and He will do it for you! Give Him the Glory, because those aggravations were to make you. If that

I can't take one more thing!

thing hadn't ever happened to me, I would have never changed. Know who you are in Him, through Him and because of Him. Your first and last name shall be known to the world. You are the Son of God; the daughter of righteousness and the covering of His grace is upon you.

Job 2:4, "And Satan answered the LORD, and said, Skin for skin, yea, all that a man hath will he give for his life." Have you ever imagined peeling a layer of your skin off? I know it may sound gross, but can you imagine it? It sounds like a horror movie. Well, that is what Satan said when he was speaking skin for skin, all that a man have will he give for his life. How much are you willing to give for your life? When one goes through the wringer and comes out as a survivor, it makes them more durable. Their skin becomes tougher and tougher. Perhaps, Satan comes after true believers to see how much they would give up for The Almighty. How much are you willing to give up, to receive double for your trouble? How much is The Most High worth to you? Is He worth a layer of skin and how much are you willing to tear off

I can't take one more thing!

to prove your loyalty to The Almighty? Stop letting Satan hold your prosperity for ransom, pay up! Skin for skin.

Job 21:6, "Even when I remember I am afraid, and trembling taketh hold on my flesh." When the strongholds of your life are stronger than you, then you need the immediate strength you have never known. You need the strength of a Shield to protect you from the fiery darts of life. You need a mountain Rock, to cover you when the forces of the enemy are roaring against you and the Oil of your Butter to give you sliding ability. A King that can give you precise direction, lead you out of the pattern of destruction; also, a Shepherd to look after you when you are headed in harm's way. He is a Judge that will correct you when you are inconceivably wrong; a Refuge that will fight your battle during the times you give up. He has a Fortress of power that you can gain victorious strength of the highest capacity. He is an Avenger to avenge your death in the case of a wounded heart, and He has the power to demolish any weapon that has formed against you. Our Heavenly Father is a Creator

I can't take one more thing!

that can speak anything into existence. He is someone that has the availability that will surely deliver you out of any situation because you believed without a shadow of doubt against the enemy of confusion. He is a Miraculous Healer when the doctors tell you there is nothing that they can do because He is the Savior of all the earth. He's a Protector from all hurt, harm, danger, and evil. He is a Provider of sufficiency so that every need in your life will be bountifully met and met on time, and a Redeemer to awaken any dead thing within you so that your soul will be granted the Eternal Life promised with pure happiness and peace. He is my Prince of Peace. He is Mercy forever more and full of Grace. Also, Jesus is the truth, always showing me the way towards His marvelous Light.

I can't take one more thing!

Aggravated Assault On Your Mind

Let Your Faith Say,
"Do Not Disturb!"
~ Parice C. Parker

I can't take one more thing!

Aggravated Assault On Your Mind

CHAPTER 13
Wash Your Steps With Butter

> *"The Word Will Give You Sliding Ability, Because Quitting Is Not An Option!"*
>
> *~ Parice C. Parker*

I can't take one more thing!

CHAPTER 13

Wash Your Steps With Butter

Assaults are formed to check the vital statistics of our spiritual being. A weapon aimed at you is either going to break you or going to make you. It trains you how to function in season and out of season. Also, it prepares one to excel, even during a dysfunctional time of your life. Daily you have the liberty of making sound choices, through various weapons that take form. I know that true life does not consist of misery, hell, torment, delusional- effects, hatred, slackness, chaos, burdens, trouble, brokenness, unhappiness, fear of achievement or violated at all times. The Word of The Most High is the might of His power. The Word of The Most High comforts and gives assurance from heaven. Job was one that washed his steps in the Word, and it became the oil of his butter! Through it,

I can't take one more thing!

he gained the sliding ability. So, therefore, when trouble came he slides through. Though his grief was heavy, his burdens became light. He lived for The Word; he survived through The Word, and he overcame because of The Word. When you wash your steps in butter, you never have to worry about being stuck in a bad position. Realizing you depend on the Word you have meditated on, to bring you out! You never have to work too troublesome to get out of a bad situation, because now you trust in The Word. The oil of your butter will slide you through your troubled times, giving you the power to overcome. *Job 29:4 "As I was in the days of my youth when the secret of God was upon my tabernacle."* At a young age, he was continuously fed power through the word. He knew that mercy was in the house of God. Grace was in the house of God, and He carried his tabernacle wherever he went. Though his life was devastated, the Word was his oil. We all are going to experience terrible things at one time or another in our lives. The key is when you wash your steps with butter, by preparing your spirit for the unprepared trials that will

I can't take one more thing!

occur. God is power, and he can feed your mind hope in a hopeless situation. He will preserve you in the time of trouble. Even when we get tired and want to give up, we must keep on going. The word will kick in and slide us through. Understanding the essence of the Word will give you wisdom. Job was one that had gained much wisdom for everything he had to go through. *Hebrew 4:16 "Let us, therefore, come boldly unto the throne of grace, that we may obtain mercy, and find grace to help in the time of need."* Job needed sympathy when his body wracked with pain. He needed mercy when his children died and when his livestock destroyed, he called mercy. When you get between a rock and a bad situation in life, God will melt that situation and allow you to slide through. Job had to slide through many bad situations. Though he had lost everything he had, he had to place his mind in a higher position than the state of his life. He placed it in The Most High and knew God was going to deliver him. He was in a very weak state of his life, and he depended on the height of the Word to be the lifter of his head! He carried a heavy load, more weight than

I can't take one more thing!

you or I could probably bare. Still, he held on. He was hurting and surely devastated. He had to keep his mind on The Most High. During rough times, you still must stay focused. Most people continue to allow their mind to stay aggravated because they meditate on the bad. The more you think about your troubles, especially the things you have no power to change. It can destroy your faith. If your faith is destroyed, so is the possibility of your fortune. Never meditate on trouble, but on the heavenly powers. Whatever can make things all possible in your life, those are the things you meditate. Ponder on your, yes! When one gets in the worst state of their life and lose everything they had, one must know that God is going to give them better than before. For everything we lose, God will replace double fold. That is how He works, as long as one hold to His Word. That is one thing that will never go void, His word. Often we look for many ways out as we are going through, but there is only one way to make it, and it is to go through. Getting tired during your process is not an option! Too many people get tired and quit. All along, they still must through! So,

I can't take one more thing!

why to waste valuable time. Crank it up and keep the faith. Only, your faith shall cause you to triumph! *Job 30:15 "Did not he that made me in the womb make him? And did not one fashion us in the womb."* For the way you are born into this world is not the way you have to leave this world. We are born into a world of sin and shaped in iniquity. Let go and let GOD perform His state of the art miracles through you. God is clothing you with his righteousness. Sometimes, He will allow many wrong things to come upon our life just to fashion us in His righteousness, as He did Job. If you dwell on your weapon, then it will soon consume you. Right now is the time to pray in the power of GOD. Even Jesus had weapons formed against Him, He too came through with all power in His hands. Your might through the strength of The Most High is numerous if you allow your hands to perform within.

Let not your heart become troubled, though you may be walking in the shadow of death, GOD has you covered. You must put all your trust in Him! Often we tend to hold onto the things that we think we have the

I can't take one more thing!

power to change but don't. You have to put 100% of your trust in Him, and then you can receive a 100 fold return. *Psalms 23:1 The Lord is your Shepard regardless of the time of the day or even in the midnight hour.* One thing about GOD is that His power never sleeps nor will it slumber. He hears your cry and knows of your needs. Think about Daniel in the loins den. We are all aware that his situation seemed hopeless. Though God closed the lion's mouth, He also locked his jaws together. If Daniel had doubt of The Most High, then he would have been eaten alive. That is how most people's hope destroyed, they ponder on too many No's and get too used to things going wrong. Often many simply forget how to live a normal and good life, because they stopped believing in all things are possible! Their doubt consumed their faith in Jesus. The same manner God locked the lions' jaws, is the same manner He has locked your assailant out so that you can't be harmed. No weapon formed against you shall prosper, and every tongue that comes against you shall be condemned.

I can't take one more thing!

God bring us out of trying times, just to encourage others. *Job 21:5 "Mark me, and be astonished, and lay your hand upon your mouth."* When things in your life are upside down. God will soon allow others to be astonished. God will work out things in your life that an ordinary man cannot explain. Especially, when things appear at its worst. That is when He works at His best! Sometimes He startles our mind through the manner He blesses. I say if you have to go through just to get double for your trouble, and then slide through. Let the power of God work for you. Job knew the day would come that his faith was going to put on trial. Still, he knew he had to stand. When the winds blow harder in life, things will devastate you and get all out of place. Remember, The Most High are on your side. Keep your mind stayed on the good things of life through the power of The Most High. Do not let your troubling times get the best of you, but get the best out of them. It is time for you to wash your steps with butter and be astonished! *Job 29:6, "When I washed my steps with butter, and the rock poured me out rivers of oil."* Increase your standing ability and fight

I can't take one more thing!

to stay alive. Get away from enemy territory. When you notice the enemy stay out of sight, they want to destroy you. Anyone that has the power to destroy you do not let them know your next move. Sometimes an enemy will be watching you and expect you to move forward, when they feed you need. Nevertheless, do not get caught up and do not trust them. Especially, if they possess enemy characteristics and could destroy you.

Sometimes we think we are in the clear as we are being delivered. But, we are not. Many run too soon and have not been strengthened adequately. Once you have been delivered from something, you must allow yourself proper time to become fully charged or else you may get caught off guard. You must be able to prove to your assailant that they are no match for you. Only The Almighty has the power to save you from your Aggravated Assaults. Know what God you serve at all times and let The Most High live larger in you, as you develop to your fullness.

I can't take one more thing!

Job 5:17, "Behold, happy is the man whom God correcteth: therefore despise not thou the chastening of the Almighty:" Let GOD know that you are happy living in bad conditions and that you are not worried! Consider it all for your good and know that valuable lessons are learned out of bad situations. Make yourself available unto His magnificent presence. Get down on your knees and ask no one to bother you. Find a place and commune with Him in prayer. Release all your troubles unto Him and do not let your heart be troubled afterward! Give yourself to Him in prayer, in a manner that you never have before. Give no thought to what you are going to pray, just pray without ceasing. During your prayer with Him, let no one interfere. Begin to rebuke everything in the name of JESUS and cause peace to overtake you and your surrounding area. Let your tongue form in the power of GOD, just let Him have His way with you. Continue to pray, until you have felt His presence and you know that he has heard your prayer.

This is a serious road that you are traveling. It will lead you towards your fulfillment in life. Realize

I can't take one more thing!

people you love will tremendously hurt you, but do not let your heart be discouraged or your faith be disturbed! The people you want to depend on, they will be dressed in sheep's clothing. Wolves are waiting to kill you. People that will commend you, really hate you. They are only nice because others are watching. When I went through my terrible times, I still did not walk alone and had been able to depend on people I thought would be by my side. I was able to depend on The WORD! I cannot turn my back on the ONE that has washed my steps with butter. He knew some things I had to step in, some things I had to step over but I kept on stepping. You must keep on stepping, regardless of what's before you. *Job 5:19 "He shall deliver thee in six troubles: yea in seven there shall be no evil touch thee."* If Job believed that after the six troubles he would be delivered, and the seven evil would not touch him, then I believed the same. After all, headaches do not last all the time. I desired to get to the point of seven when my troubles would be over. *Job 5:21 "Thou shalt be hidden from the scourge of the tongue: neither shalt thou is afraid*

I can't take one more thing!

of destruction when it cometh." There is a certain point in life when we all must mature spiritually. Speaking, grow up in the WORD. *Job 12:13 "With him is wisdom and strength, he hath counsel and understanding."* You will receive instruction from GOD on how to get out and make it through. He is teaching you how to survive! His voice of comfort will speak to you, and His WORD will guide you through. Nothing can or will invade the voice of the Lord; you will hear loud and clear. His voice is amazingly strong and all-powerful. His voice awakens every sense and brings effectiveness into place. What if I had been disobedient to His voice or too lazy to write? Apparently, you would not be reading this book right now; what If I had let all my struggles and trials keep me from continuing to complete this book? I would not know my purpose or be living in it. Or what if I would have quit when I finished my first writings, then it would not have been a complete book? It is valuable and life threatening for us to listen and ACT IN OBEDIENCE. Just as we begin a comprehensive work, we must finish. We should never allow life's

I can't take one more thing!

troubles to interfere with a divine assignment or tear us from our belief. Furthermore, or cause us to stop. When He tells you to do something, complete it. Do not allow it to finish. Regardless of what may occur, finish His assignment at all times! *Job 33:37 "God thundereth marvelously with his voice; great things doeth he, which we cannot comprehend."* His voice sounds louder than any trumpet that has ever blown and is sympathetically soothing to your heart. Your sense of blindness is immediately unfolded; your sight is then made whole. Your ears will hear clearer than they have. Besides, the touch of the true SPIRIT of Jesus will caress your heart, with warmth of assurance. No doubt will overwhelm you. You will be sure of your right now task. *Job 33:4 "The Spirit of God hath made me, and the breath of the Almighty hath given me life."* Listen! Job felt His presence as He was fed the WORD. You must feel what your assignment is. We might get many ideas, but there is one vision that will be for sure in your heart. Also, it will not work until it moves within you. You must feel it! It will rest on your mind and your nights will become restless

I can't take one more thing!

until it manifests! Then, will you know it was from The Most High! Even He will not let you rest until it is complete. Perhaps, it could be the cause of your many aggravations. Once you move forward in it, there will be a known effect, and you will know. Your aggravation could be an answer to the next move you are required to make. Notice, once you are aggravated it makes you more aware. Remember, He works mysteriously! God's sheep will know His voice. Job was one that heard from the voice of the Lord. Though sometimes we may get troubled in life, we must move forward as God speaks to us. *John 10:15 "As the Father knoweth me, even so know I the Father: and I lay down my life for the sheep."*

If Jesus took the time to come into this world to save a wretch like you and me, then He deserves the utmost respect He had the entire heavenly host working through Him, with Him and for Him. That is why He is so powerful. Can you imagine if your family or friends would cooperate with you instead of against you? Could you imagine the strength you could have and how well your vision would speak?

I can't take one more thing!

What about the enemies that try to attack. The more you have to work for you, the less you have used to work for you and the easier it is to make it. Jesus has a host of heavenly powers, and He wants to share them all with you. Isn't that worth holding on to? An entire host of heaven, waiting to fulfill your life! WOW! I believed that Job tapped into heavenly powers that are why he was able to hold on. His eyes must have seen what was before him, and he knew he could not go back. So, he held on. Look back over your life at all you have experienced, is it worth a step forward? Or are you willing to stay in a comatose state? If you want double for your trouble, I know you will not find it moving backward. However, you will do as you progress and reach higher! Know that The WORD is all powerful and will give you sliding ability because quitting is not an option!

Job's faith was authenticated as he endured. Some people have a low tolerance level. However, Job's was high. Though he hurt and was in pain, he tolerated it well. After the complaints, you still must go through. Be strong, hold your head up and stand with dignity.

I can't take one more thing!

Job 21:6, "Even when I remember I am afraid, and trembling taketh hold on my flesh." When the strongholds of your life are stronger than you, then you need the immediate strength you have never known. You need the strength of a Shield to protect you from the fiery darts of life. You need a mountain Rock, to cover you when the forces of the enemy are roaring against you and the Oil of your Butter to give you sliding ability. A King that can give you perfect direction, lead you out of the pattern of destruction; also, a Shepherd to look after you when you are headed in harm's way. He is a Judge that will correct you when you are inconceivably wrong; a Refuge that will fight your battle during the times you give up. He has a Fortress of power that you can gain victorious strength of the highest capacity. He is an Avenger to avenge your death in the case of a wounded heart, and He has the power to demolish any weapon that has formed against you. Our Heavenly Father is a Creator that can speak anything into existence. He is someone that has the availability that will surely deliver you out of any situation because you believed without a

I can't take one more thing!

shadow of doubt against the enemy of confusion. He is a Miraculous Healer when the doctors tell you there is nothing that they can do because He is the Savior of all the earth. He's a Protector from all hurt, harm, danger, and evil. He is a Provider of sufficiency so that every need in your life will be bountifully met and met on time, and a Redeemer to awaken any dead thing within you so that your soul will be granted the Eternal Life promised with pure happiness and peace. He is my Prince of Peace. He is Mercy forever more and full of Grace. Also, Jesus is the truth, always showing me the way towards His marvelous Light.

I can't take one more thing!

Aggravated Assault On Your Mind

"Let Your Captivity, Make Your Provision!"

~Parice C. Parker

I can't take one more thing!

Aggravated Assault On Your Mind

CHAPTER 14
The Return of Captivity

"Once Captive, Now Free!"

~ Parice. C. Parker

I can't take one more thing!
CHAPTER 14

The Return of Captivity

When you endure a large trial, He will make sure that all the world knows that He brought you through. Once He put His seal on you, nothing can tamper with its safety! You become His authentically! Heaven will be your guarantee, and you must represent all qualities so that heaven can back you up. The goods you will contain will be astonishing. The Heavenly Host will stand your guard! So, therefore, quitting is not an option. *Job 37:7 "He sealeth up the hand of every man; that all men may know his work."* Regardless of any weapons that form against you, stand and obtain your victory. Job was one that stood firm as he suffered patiently. Often, many suffer and go through terrible times. Although they are suffering, how well do they represent The Almighty? Many things you

I can't take one more thing!

must learn how to tolerate, especially when you can see your end. If you serve The Most High, you should know that your latter will be far greater than your beginning. There is a time to expect greatness to flourish in your life. The things you once could not tolerate, you will be driven to endure. Do not allow your sufferings to be in vain. I do not know of anyone that has stood firm on The WORD and forsaken! There is not one! Once one stands firm being unmovable, rewards must take its rightful place. Always keep in mind that His WORD is His bond. Nothing can stick closer together, and they are inseparable, not even super glue. So, therefore, if His WORD has to present itself to you for a return. Stand on it till it comes to pass. During Job's endurance, he grew mightily in patience. People are watching you as you endure. Be careful what you show them. A complaining spirit will get you nowhere. Neither putting blame on others nor pouting just to get your way. Grow up and mature in patience! Stop blaming others and begin to take responsibility for yourself without having a pity party. Stand on His WORD and

I can't take one more thing!

cause your faith to deliver you. Smile, because your faith is on candid camera.

Job 42:10 "And the Lord turned the captivity of Job when he prayed for his friends: Also the LORD gave Job twice as much as he had before." Many went to Job, prosecuted him and scorned his name. Still, he bowed down on their behalf and asked the Lord to forgive them. When you grow in a spiritual manner, your heart will be increased with heavenly love. The Spirit of God will forever be with you. Job did not treat others how they treated him. He prayed for them, through it all. Not everyone is looking through their spiritual eyes nor can they see what you can. That is where your heart needs to bow on their behalf. Though I was angry with many that went against me. I could not hold them ruggedly in my heart. I prayed that God would reach their hearts in places I could never reach. Nevertheless, He touched them and changed me. We must pray for one another's imperfections. Perhaps, that may be the one thing holding your blessings in contempt. Job gained a double portion for everything he lost. Simply, because He prayed for his friends. The

I can't take one more thing!

ones that prosecuted his faith. He showed God His heart. Job always washed his steps in butter. He helped those that were poor looked after the fatherless, and loved everyone. He showed others the way to God. He welcomed everyone and blessed many. He supplied many with goodness as he showed them mercy. He simply washed his steps in butter. He sowed unusual seeds through showing others God. Show God the love you have in your heart and He will show you double in return. *Job 5:19 "He shall deliver thee in six troubles: yea in seven there shall be no evil touch thee."*

God wants to bless you beyond recognition and He will. No matter who or what has aggravated your life, love them anyway. When you have the love of The Most High working on the inside of you, He will work amazingly in your life. Job was covered before He went through and his increase was doubled as he came out. It is time that you expect double for all your troubles. God simply wants you to be happy. Pray for happiness, because everything you went through has been a part of making you. God used your life to prove to Satan that you are authentically His. Also, He loses

I can't take one more thing!

absolutely nothing. He is going to multiply your life with everything you ever wanted and desired. He is a God that blesses in abundance. No man will be able to count your worth. Be blessed and know that God is who He says He is. Once God delivered Job, no evil was ever able to touch Him again. That is the exact point that God wants for our life. He wants us to be untouchable. Absolutely nothing will ever have power over you or your life again. Your life will become untouchable to the enemy. Afterward, Job lived an untouchable life. Expect The Most High to deliver you to live an untouchable life from all evil. Once a seal is put on you, nothing can go in unless the seal was broken. The Most High never breaks His WORD; His bond will cover you and take you into eternity with Him. Satan will no longer be able to put curses on one that is proved to be ready. All that you tolerate for a purpose is proof that you are willing and capable of all that is due to you. *Job 42:12 &13 "So the Lord blessed the latter end of Job more than his beginning: and he had fourteen thousand sheep, and six thousand camels, and a thousand yoke of oxen, and a thousand*

I can't take one more thing!

she-asses. He also had seven sons and three daughters, what a huge loss." The Almighty knew Job's outcome as He went into his many life assaults. However, he was only proving Job. Be blessed and be untouchable as you're proofed! Understand the reason while you were held captive for so long and get your return! The return of captivity should reward one greatly!

Job 21:6, "Even when I remember I am afraid, and trembling taketh hold on my flesh." When the strongholds of your life are stronger than you, then you need the immediate strength you have never known. You need the strength of a Shield to protect you from the fiery darts of life. You need a mountain Rock, to cover you when the forces of the enemy are roaring against you and the Oil of your Butter to give you sliding ability. A King that can give you perfect direction, lead you out of the pattern of destruction; also, a Shepherd to look after you when you are headed in harm's way. He is a Judge that will correct you when you are inconceivably wrong; a Refuge that will fight your battle during the times you give up. He

I can't take one more thing!

has a Fortress of power that you can gain victorious strength of the highest capacity. He is an Avenger to avenge your death in the case of a wounded heart, and He has the power to demolish any weapon that has formed against you. Our Heavenly Father is a Creator that can speak anything into existence. He is someone that has the availability that will surely deliver you out of any situation because you believed without a shadow of doubt against the enemy of confusion. He is a Miraculous Healer when the doctors tell you there is nothing that they can do because He is the Savior of all the earth. He's a Protector from all hurt, harm, danger, and evil. He is a Provider of sufficiency so that every need in your life will be bountifully met and met on time, and a Redeemer to awaken any dead thing within you so that your soul will grant the Eternal Life promised with pure happiness and peace. He is my Prince of Peace. He is Mercy forever more and full of Grace. Also, Jesus is the truth, always showing me the way towards His marvelous Light.

I can't take one more thing!

Spiritual Dedication to the ones who believed in me:

Special dedication to my Precious Heavenly Father that sits high and looked so low to see me. I love you Father for all that you have done; furthermore, for being God over my life. I love you for allowing the Anointed Blood of your only begotten son to save my soul. Jesus, I will forever be in debt to you for saving such a person as I, with a generous love from my heart to yours always, Thank you, LORD. I thank The Most High God for allowing me to have this beautiful gift that you have entrusted me. You did it all; you thought that much of me and I pray that this book, in the name of Jesus, will touch every heart, change every life and will cause a chain reaction for many to abide in you. Father, I dedicate this book to you, because you dedicated Jesus to me, and every vessel that reads it. I pray that they become more dedicated to you. I love you Lord and in you, I claim the victory for all the captives to be set free, in Jesus

I can't take one more thing!

name I pray. Amen, Amen & Amen, I love you, LORD.

I can't take one more thing!

Aggravated Assault on Your Mind

What inspired me to write this book?

One night I was so angry with everything that life had to offer, I grew mad at the world. I was helping everyone that did not care. My love was abused and kindness used. When you sit down and see your life for what it is, often, one will realize they've

I can't take one more thing!

messed up! As I was trying to live right, everything was trying to cause my faith to turn around. Fury will cause you to rise to the point of no return! Once I felt the rage of my assault, I desired to become a victorious champion. It was simply time to introduce my assailant to The Most High in my life. My author and finisher of my faith, Jesus! That aggravation was the beginning of a new strength in me, and through it I received the gift of inspirational writing!

I pray this book highly encourages you to become greater than you ever imagined!

Authentically Made,
Apostle, Parice Parker

Ephesians 3:7, Whereof I was made a minister, According to the gift of the grace of God given unto me by the effectual working of his power.

I can't take one more thing!

Dedications to the special people in my life:

All that was present in my life during hard times and remained, showing love.

My heart says, "thank you!"

I can't take one more thing!

Other Inspirational Books by Parice Parker

- *Living Life in A Messed Up Situation Volume One*
- *Living Life in A Messed Up Situation Volume Two*
- *A Precious Gift from God*
- *The Anointing Powers of Your Hands*
- *Word Wonders*
- *The Birth of an Author Shall Be Born*
- *From Eating Crumbs to Transforming Life*
- *Live Laugh Love & Be Happy*
- *Breaking the Back of Poverty (Book)*
- *Breaking the Back of Poverty (Journal)*
- *Power to Push You*

I can't take one more thing!

To Order Inspirational Books by Parice Parker please visit her online bookstore

www.pariceparker.biz

CEO of Fountain of Life Publisher's House

The House of Transformation Miracle Ministries or Fountain of Life Empowerment Ministries

Please Mail All Correspondence

To: P. O Box 922612 Norcross GA 30010

Attention: Apostle Parice Parker

I can't take one more thing!

Aggravated Assault On Your Mind

Phenomenal: Have you ever felt, the very person you have surely loved or believed in has attacked you? It may have been your closest friend, relative, child, your spouse or even yourself. Sometimes you wanted to cry and could not. Shortly afterwards, while gazing about the pain immediately tears began to fall as a flowing river. Your heart has been assaulted and snared with claws of intentions to kill. A multitude of thoughts circulate in your mind and then you began to say to yourself **"How did I let this happen to me?"** Your situation was bound to occur, because somewhere along the way you have allowed your circumstance to control your mind. Allegedly, you put your trust in the wrong one or thing and then you are thrown off

I can't take one more thing!

guard. Most definitely, you wonder, who do I blame? You did not realize you have entrusted so much of your heart to be assaulted through the passion of love you have given. A since of blindness has overwhelmed your thinking ability, rearranging your life, and throwing it off balance. Truly, there is an explanation and an apology due, but none is ever given. Certainly, you have tried to generate an effectual change. Perhaps, the more you have tried, the more your relationship seemed to die. **Instantly thinking, What Is The Use?**

I can't take one more thing!

A Precious Gift from God

Talent Is Too Good To Waste
Parice C Parker

Your Gift Discovery? It teaches one the value of their natural born talent and motivates one to Live Life On Purpose! This book inspires the heart, gives courage to your *How to Ability* and causes you to live in the pursuit of your happiness. Every natural born leader needs to read this book, it is **AWE – INSPIRING!**

I can't take one more thing!

Living Life In A Messed Up Situation
Volume One

Powerful: God will assign the most in-depth spiritual cleaning service through the Blood of Jesus the Christ to clean up your messed up life. **Every messed up situation that you are living** in will have a **Sparkling Effect** when God gets finished with you. Some things He dusts off, others He wipes down and some need to be polished to shine.

I can't take one more thing!

Get Polished Perfect after reading this book and simply gain it all.

I can't take one more thing!

The Birth of An Author Shall Be Born

Fascinating ... Dazing at the fact you have a book inside and don't know where to start or how to get it out! This book have dynamic key points and great strategies on how to succeed in book writing from start to finish. It's time to discover the author in you and to **GET THAT BOOK OUT Of YOU!** This book is full of techniques to motivate the author inside... The Birth of an Author Shall Be Born, Is It YOU?

I can't take one more thing!

Word Wonders

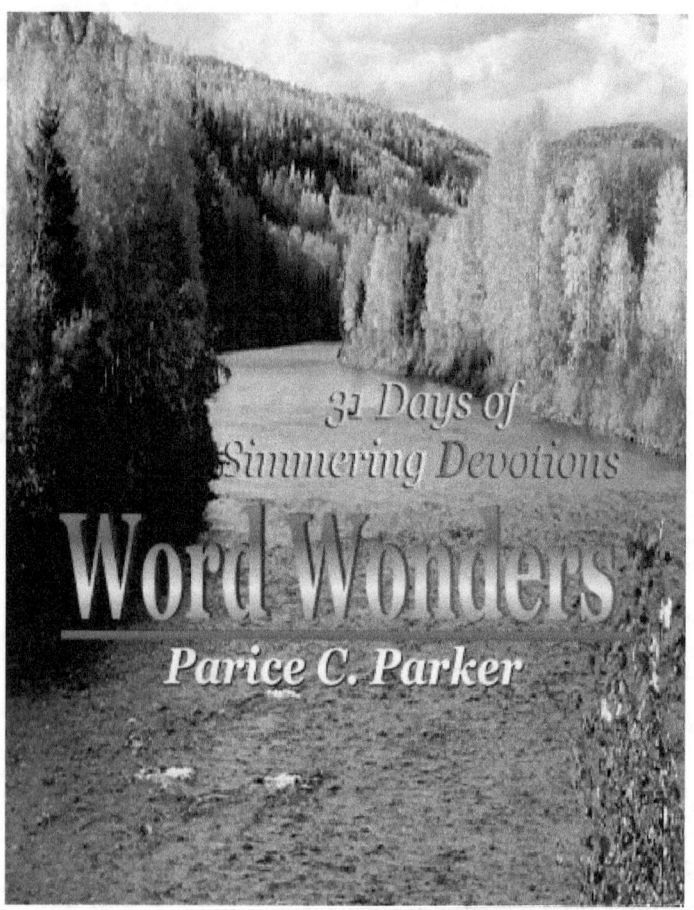

A Eye – Opening ... Word Wonder inspires your HOPE to Greatly Influence your FAITH and it's a magnificent daily devotional book to help keep you focused in word. It EMPOWERS Positive Powers to cause DIVINE FAVOR to ABOUND TOWARDS YOU! Simple things you need to be equipped with more favor from on high. Get This Book TODAY!

I can't take one more thing!

From Eating Crumbs To Transforming Wealth

***Riveting* ...** Finally, a book that keeps you in a thriving mental state that causes your HOPE to burst through! Now, it is time to identify the real you by introducing the TROPHY that is Hidden inside. It's your time to stop eating the crumbs of life and Indulge In Your WEALTHY Place!

I can't take one more thing!

The Anointing Powers of Your Hands

Absorbing ...The Anointing Powers of Your Hands has the ability to cause you to ***REACH*** for Dreams even You Thought They Were Impossible! It Motivates that **IMPOSSIBLE VISION TO COME TO PASS** and it places it in your **Rear View Mirror!**

I can't take one more thing!

Power to Push You

Military Force ... When you fix your mind on the power to excel and purpose to hit the target, then it is a done deal. Your goal is now to achieve. No one,

I can't take one more thing!

nothing or tiredness could stop you now. Power to Push You is missioned to cause you to be an eye specialist. Your eyes will begin to see the benefits of vision; the aspirations once accomplished, and you will have an **IMPEMTUOUS ZEAL.** No one can dream for this vision as you or push it in the manner you can and stay focused as you. Vision is the power to drive people but first one must see the fullness, must feel the passion for it to live and have an **IMPEMTUOUS ZEAL** to birth it. Vision is a life modifier and life decorator. It can give you a complete makeover from inside out. Also, when others see it, they will want to be a part or some of what you have. Your success will cause others to desire a much better life and give others a fresh hope to accomplish. Power to Push You speaks for itself and all that connects and read Power to Push You shall cause their visions to exist. It's a **DYNOMITE PUSHER!**

I can't take one more thing!

Live Love Laugh & Be Happy

It's like medicine to your bones ...
Parice Parker

Live Love Laugh & Be Happy *Fabulous* ... Daily many live life being terribly unhappy wanting others to really care but, are too often overlooked. It's time you get a new ray of hope. A time for healing inside and out. Live Love Laugh & Be Happy is purposed to expose new life to your everyday living. Your laughter is on its way, because those that sow in tears of sorrow, shall reap in tears of joy!

I can't take one more thing!

Fountain of Life Publishers House

P. O. Box 922612, Norcross, GA 30010
Phone: 404.936.3989

For book orders or wholesale distribution
Website: www.pariceparker.biz

I can't take one more thing!

www.ingramcontent.com/pod-product-compliance
Lightning Source LLC
Chambersburg PA
CBHW071759300426
44116CB00009B/1138